My Beautiful Game

My Beautiful Game

Nancy Dell'Olio

BANTAM PRESS

LONDON • TORONTO • SYDNEY • AUCKLAND • JOHANNESBURG

TRANSWORLD PUBLISHERS
61–63 Uxbridge Road, London W5 5SA
A Random House Group Company
www.booksattransworld.co.uk

First published in Great Britain
in 2007 by Bantam Press
an imprint of Transworld Publishers

A CIP catalogue record for this book
is available from the British Library.

ISBN 9780593059050 (cased)
9780593059067 (tpb)

Extract from 'Football in the Trenches' by Stuart Butler reproduced by
kind permission of www.footballpoets.org. Copyright © Stuart Butler 2000.
Extract on p. 239 from 'The Absurd Man' by Albert Camus in *The Myth of Sisyphus and Other
Essays*, published by Penguin, London, 1955. Original essay published by Librairie Gallimard.

Addresses for Random House Group Ltd companies outside the UK
can be found at: www.randomhouse.co.uk
The Random House Group Ltd Reg. No. 954009

The Random House Group Ltd makes every effort to ensure that the papers used in its books
are made from trees that have been legally sourced from well-managed and credibly certified
forests. Our paper procurement policy can be found at: www.randomhouse.co.uk/paper.htm

Typeset in 11½/17½pt Granjon by
Falcon Oast Graphic Art Ltd.

Printed and bound in Great Britain by
Clays Ltd, Bungay, Suffolk

2 4 6 8 10 9 7 5 3 1

For Sven . . . with whom I shared this journey,
for Ilena, my niece, who brings new love and
light to my future, and for all those I love.

CONTENTS

•

PROLOGUE

•

Life has only one true attraction, which is the attraction of the game: but only if we do not care if we lose or win.

BAUDELAIRE

SOMETIMES IT TAKES JUST A SINGLE MOMENT TO MAKE US realize fully what it is to be alive – and nothing can shock us more profoundly into that awareness than suddenly coming face to face with death. So it was for me at twenty-one, the coming of age and two years before graduation, that the unconscious moment of a drunken driver, no more than the careless toss of his cigarette butt, changed my life for ever.

The front door of my parents' villa in Apulia opened directly on to the village high street. As I stepped out into the road I had not a care in the world. The white Fiat came out of nowhere on the wrong side of the road. I never knew what hit me. No memory of the impact remains. But in my darker moments I replay the horror of the accident in my imagination like an animal worrying at a wound. I imagine the impact of the car on a human body – the inanimate against the living thing. And I realize how fragile we are – and yet so resilient.

The trauma of the accident has faded, but the experience of being near to death has never left me. Being in a coma was like being lost between two worlds. As I recovered consciousness I remember the clear light that led me out of that dark void; I was like a lost girl catching sight of her mother. The feeling of being guided has been with me ever since. Since the accident, my memories are often elusive, and the times I remember most vividly are the times when I was most aware. Like awakening from being locked in a coma, to me being alive is being fully conscious.

What we call a beginning is often an end and, strangely, the end is often where we start from. So my beginning will tell the story of the end of England's dream in Germany in 2006, with all the anguish and heartache it brought. The scar of what happened and the knowledge of what might have been remains with all of those involved. And the end for England meant another new beginning for me.

Although I fell in love with a football manager, my life is not defined by football. The game has become a passion for me, but it is by no means my reason to be. I have had the opportunity of a unique viewpoint on the English game over the last five years. I love the characters and personalities in English football; you will not find their like anywhere in the world. As one of several parallel themes in the writing of this autobiography, I will enjoy expressing my own unconventional views on the game and have no fear in voicing observations that Sven would never make. So, as *caveat lector* to all, be warned that my opinions are all my own and I take no responsibility for any offence I may cause to oversensitive egos in the game. Self-interested individuals have exploited 'the beautiful game'. Both its nature and its governance changed over my time in the UK.

In telling my story I have tried to be honest, although there is always room for self-delusion in recounting the cut and thrust of life in the public eye, especially in love and football. Some people I have known well and can make a judgement from having seen them in the round and from my own direct experience. Others I do not know so well and am only able to describe from limited impressions or a brief encounter. We mostly judge ourselves by our intentions and others by their actions. The intentions of others are more or less invisible, while their actions are right in our faces. My actions have often been misread by others who have not understood my intentions. I will allow others the same comfort by readily admitting that I may also be wrong in my interpretation of what they have done.

The twelve chapters in this book do not represent the whole of my story. They do reflect the unfolding of my life as seen from a perspective after my turbulent years in England. As an American-Italian (my education was that way round), a Jew and a Roman Catholic, I feel that the exotic cocktail of my life has been shaken not stirred by my Anglophile's perspective and my five years crazy in love with London. After such an initiation I think I am entitled to call myself a cosmopolitan woman and a citizen of the world. I believe in the new internationalism and hope that the story of my life living out of a suitcase will be a testament to the positive influence of openness and greater globalization. Of all the great cities of the world, I feel most affinity with Rome. I love the people, the food, the history and the architecture. For me as a European, my Roman classical heritage is the profound cultural climate in which I live and breathe. It is also the greatest city of romance, and it was there that I met both my ex-husband and Sven-Goran Eriksson.

I am a sucker for love. My film archive is full of Audrey Hepburn and the heart of this book is my discovery of love and my love affair with life. From my infancy and early child-hood in America through my school and university days (when some friends called me a bluestocking), I have always believed in Romance. Even when I fell in love, hurt others and got hurt, I have always believed that personal growth requires the emotional crucible of love to reach maturity. This is where the nature of women comes into its own. Women understand the selflessness of love in a way that men do not. Their biology is different, and so much of the journey of love is in realizing the differences and managing them in our relationships.

My welcome to public life and the front page in England was not quite how I had imagined it would be. It is always a little devastating (see, I have learned the English art of under-statement) for a girl when her man sits on the edge of the bed and tells her 'there is something in the papers today you should know about.' Of course this is an old story – and a perfectly bloody one when you are living your life in public – but we southern European women are made of strong stuff and are very practical in the love department, knowing that a man can seldom resist temptation. Much of the Sven and Nancy story was a romance that happened before we ever came to England. We had both been through pain before. My love for Sven caused the break-up of my first marriage – a prospect I could not have imagined before we met or even at first meeting. Falling in love with a cool Swede (although I assure you this is only his public persona) did not happen overnight and by nature I am not unfaithful. In this account, after much soul-searching, I am breaking my silence of the last six years to tell my side of the story. I am uneasy leaving the legacy of our life and times in England to the witness of tabloid columns, and I am grateful for a chance to give my perspective.

The English media is a big beast and has swallowed up some of the brightest and most talented minds in the country. All humans love to gossip – we kid ourselves if we think any differently – but we often fall below our better selves in our blind fascination for tabloid culture, which is really a form of voyeurism. However, if you live your life in the public eye you must expect what comes with the territory. To my mind an admission and a confession can be forgiven with dignity. Sven may well have deceived me but he never lied to me. The affairs happened, but they were not the vicious scandals presented in the turbocharged tabloids. I will never fully understand what was going on in his mind or why he made the choices he made, though affairs are often a man's way of attracting attention. But behind the volatile nature of our relationship lay a real strength, so that whatever others there may have been made no difference to the deep love and supreme affection we have for each other.

I will leave Sven's story to his own autobiography. We may have to wait a long time for that. But where a relationship has been lived in public there is a need for truth. Only forgiveness can free those with a conscience from the consequences of unbecoming conduct. It is often easier for others to forgive you than for you to forgive yourself. Sven has had to say sorry many times in his life – on several occasions to me and also to England. And when Sven says sorry he definitely means it. Moving on is not easy for any of us after six years. There is a hole in our hearts where England used to be and still a sense of a mission unfulfilled. The end of a dream is hard enough to endure when you suffer in private; a very public humiliation is so much more difficult to bear, although it can give you an insight into yourself. Being selected as the England manager was one of Sven's proudest moments, not fulfilling the dream his greatest disappointment.

Falling in love with a man who lives for football from the front benches, I have had to follow the ball to many places and watch many matches. I have learned that the rules of the game are the key to harmony. Playing by the rules makes a riot into a competition, and by teamwork players learn to cooperate to win. Like life, this gives a unique experience to those who play and those who watch. When I read the lines of the football poet and historian Stuart Butler and learned the amazing story of the First World War Christmas truce in 1914, I saw the game in a new light and for the first time understood how football could become a force for world change:

> *They embraced in No Man's Land and football*
> *Harmonized the nations' animosities;*
> *And what if the playing of the people's game*
> *Had continued beyond that Christmas time?*

I have been so lucky and blessed to have lived a charmed life. I wish it could be the same for every child. My disillusionment with political life left me searching for my personal meaning and for a way to give to others, less fortunate than myself, a feeling of hope – like the light of love that led me out of my coma. The idea for Truce International was born within a small circle of our close friends who believe with me and Sven that the power of world football could be mobilized behind the United Nations as a new force for world peace. We arrived in England as a new wave of violence and war escalated all around the world. After 9/11 and war in Iraq, we decided to champion the cause of football for peace. World peace is still a dream, but if the simple act of kicking a ball can help to ease just one finger on a trigger, I am content. You have my invitation to 'Kick a Ball for Peace'.

THE LAST GAME

•

You must dare to fail if you are to dare to succeed.

SVEN-GORAN ERIKSSON

THE FIFTH PENALTY: CRISTIANO RONALDO CROSSES HIMSELF and steps up to the ball with all the implicit assurance of faith. Another twist of fate that the crucial strike will be taken by the man whom England fans are already blaming for the dismissal of our impetuous star striker, Wayne Rooney, in the sixty-second minute for allegedly treading Ricardo Carvalho in the groin. There is a sense of déjà vu in the box and on the tense faces in the England stands – not just a flashback to Portugal 2004 but to an earlier World Cup quarter-final against Argentina in 1998. That had also ended in defeat on penalties after David Beckham had suffered a similar dismissal. A hush falls on the crowd as Ronaldo keys up. I have a sense of impending doom. I know that if he scores, the kick that sends England out of the World Cup will be the last kick of Sven's last game in charge. Ronaldo hesitates for a fraction of a second. Then, with the sure, instinctive precision of one of the world's finest strikers, he powers the ball into the net and Paul Robinson is left standing as if in the face of the inevitable.

In less time than the closing of an eyelid, the dream was over. The shock was mind-numbing. This was the end of the dream for me, for my adopted country of five years, for my partner, for his captain, and the end of all those hopes for England's young and gifted star players.

I will never forget the pain of the moment that defined the fate of England's national team. My life in England seemed to replay in my mind's eye, and the realization that this chapter of my life was at an end welled up like the tears I could not hold back. And yet it had all seemed so different that morning as we set out from the Brenner's Park Hotel in Baden-Baden. The mood was one of quiet optimism. Sven's son and daughter, Johan and Lina, and I decided to travel together by limousine. As we left, the England camp was buoyant and the team eager for a chance to even the score with Portugal.

There had been nerves in the build-up to the game. Over dinner, the American sports psychologist Marc-Simon Segal of the organization Winning Mind had told me of his fears about the reluctance of the squad to take the penalty practice as seriously as they should. He felt they were assuming an attitude of false bravado, which he viewed as displacement activity to avert the fear of failure. Prescient: the spectre of this penalty phobia would soon come back to haunt the England players. My own feeling is that this reflects a difference in attitude towards the game between northern and southern European cultures. The former can be too cerebral, the latter too passionate. This temperament can often be seen in the flow of games and the belief in luck or the hand of God so apparent in the South American game. Of course, in my own life, I have good first-hand experience of the attraction and clash between Latin and Nordic types!

This is *the* match. Every World Cup match is *the* match, but this is Portugal, who put England out in 2004. Every day before and after a big match is psychological torture for me. Win or lose, the result is the same in the adrenalin stakes. Hormones are firing on all cylinders from the moment your mind wakes up. I am unable to eat for the whole day before a game. The day is beautiful as we drive from Baden-Baden. The brilliant sunshine lights up the landscape like those old photographic negatives printing to positive. Johan, Lina and I are in high spirits. We are all far too nervous for a proper conversation yet too excited to stay quiet. No call from Sven – the reception on the autobahn is bad. He always calls me before every match. This is our ritual. All the stress is getting to us, so Lina and I decide to stop to freshen up and visit the Ladies. When I return, there is a missed call on my phone from Sven. Soon he will be too busy. I call back and the voicemail kicks in. I am uncomfortable leaving a message. My voice catches as I realize we may not be able to speak before the game. I suppress the fear that this might be an ill omen.

As the car enters Gelsenkirchen we assume our masks and it

is time for the play to start. The first act is the pre-match cocktail reception. I am amazed at how we can all keep up the small-talk. Just one hour and a half – ninety minutes – can change your destiny. I do a lot of kissing and greet FIFA President Sepp Blatter. He is a master of this type of charm. The cream of international football is in the room and Germany's manager Franz Beckenbauer looks on authoritatively – the World Cup is going well for Germany. Somehow, I don't feel very sociable and take refuge with Ann Thompson, wife of the FA chairman, almost colliding with Boris Becker in my haste. There is no hope now of talking to Sven. I need my seat.

If you want to see England fans at their best you need to watch England play at the World Cup. They always create a most fantastic atmosphere. Walking into the AufSchalke Arena was just as if we were playing at home, with the England supporters in the majority. No team ever had so loyal a following. I am always amazed at the roar and the wall of sound it creates – like being on an ancient battlefield. When I was living in Rome the Colosseum was at my door. The spectacle of a football stadium in full cry must be comparable to the arena long ago.

Once I am in my seat I do not like to speak. I am sitting by myself amidst the FA directors. The tension is so thick you could grate it over pasta. Doug Ellis, David Davies, David Dein and the others all surround me. It is as if the group's collective will can somehow influence the outcome of the game. I look for the familiar face of the England manager. He will be in his element!

The match starts well when a slip by Carvalho gives Rooney an early chance at goal. He is charged down. The bright start promises a hard-fought rematch between these rivals, similar to the UEFA Euro 2004 quarter-final. A Luis Figo free kick from the England box leaves England looking vulnerable. So little advantage gained by either side as we approach half-time. Then, before the second half really gets under way, David Beckham is injured and has to make way for Aaron Lennon. Is this a sign? Sven will be anxious about losing his captain at this crucial stage of the game. Then, unbelievably, a red card is shown to Wayne Rooney. We are unable to see from the stands just what has happened. Perhaps, out of frustration with his recent knee injury, Wayne just snapped. Then he is walking off the pitch and England are down to ten men. After gaining the upper hand, they will surely be forced back on to the defensive. I can hardly bear to watch and seeing both David and Wayne on the bench is the one of the most poignant moments I can remember. Yet the thin white line held on and, even with ten men, put Portugal to the test.

Then we are into extra time. The first stanza is just a blur, but the England team is doing the heroic thing that England does so well. Forwards ever and backwards never, and then we are into the end of the first half of extra time. We are all exhausted on the stands. How must it be for the players? Fifteen minutes to go and if no one scores it will be down to a penalty shoot-out. I try not to think of Marc-Simon Segal's fears for England over penalty phobia or the ill omens of the day. This is pure superstition! But I can't shake off that nervous feeling. For a moment I am distracted by the sight of Mick Jagger huddling with Franz Beckenbauer in the box. What a combination – two star-sized egos enthralled. I try not to look too hard at Sven. I feel uncomfortable watching him at a match like a stranger from afar. The game is so long. The Portuguese are running on empty and England are hanging on, desperate to push on to penalties. John Terry has cramp in his leg. I have cramp in my stomach. There is no time-wasting from England, even though we are a man down. Portugal are struggling even with a one-man advantage. They still can't finish and England are playing a strong defensive game. Nuno Maniche takes one last shot on a chance from Luis Miguel. Thank God! It's over the crossbar. At last the end of extra time and the two teams are tied. The tension could not be greater. I look at Sven, so nervously impassive, and feel like Hector's wife, powerless to help on the walls of Troy.

The penalty shoot-out. The temperature in the stadium has reached 30 degrees. England have given their all and shown the critics that we do have the passion and the staying power. Portugal lock arms in a gesture of solidarity as Simao opens the running. He rubs his hair and looks round at the stadium before shooting left. First blood to Portugal! Frank Lampard is set to take the first strike for England. He is not looking as confident as usual. England's first penalty is blocked. Portugal's next ball ricochets off the post. Still one–nil to Portugal, but England are back in. I look around the stands at the different expressions on the faces. So much expectation invested. Then, a cheer – it's England again and this time the ball is in for Hargreaves!

The tension is unbearable as Steven Gerrard then misses the next one for England. I can't believe Lampard and Gerrard have both been beaten today; this is not what we expected after their performance in the Premier League. Portugal steps up again to score. Then it is Jamie Carragher. He takes a snap spot kick for England, and then unbelievably has to take it again as the referee had not blown his whistle. All the more pressure piled on frayed nerves. The Portuguese goalkeeper dives left and stops it. England has scored one and missed three. My fingers have lost all feeling, I've been clenching them so hard. The Portuguese star striker, Ronaldo, walks forward to take up his position. He has the sure knowledge that he can put Portugal into the semi-final with this strike. The England stands are deathly quiet in the realization that everything is riding on his kick. I blink once and the ball is in the back of the net. My England is out of the World Cup.

How do you feel when you know your world is about to end? The collective deflation is suffocating. Losing any big match is a trial. When you arrive, everyone is buzzing and expectant. You win, and everyone wants to be friends and kiss and congratulate you. You lose, and there is all that awkward embarrassment and avoidance, mixed with the sly curiosity of your rivals. There is usually more internecine strife in the court of the football king than in the Bible or in Renaissance history, but on this day there is none of that – just the feeling of numbness coming from a dimension beyond emotional pain. The shock is disorientating, like an out-of-body experience. How can I make it to the car for refuge? Thank heavens there are no photographers in the box. I am trying to avoid eye contact. I know people will be looking at me for my reaction. I have only one – and that is tears.

Everyone is in tears. Distraught players, families and fans are all in the grip of a massive breakdown. How must it be for the nation? I can see Victoria Beckham sobbing and trying to comfort little Brooklyn, who is only seven. Cheryl Tweedy is trying to comfort them both and crying herself. Even the media commentators are at a loss. The players are worst hit – feeling all the shame of defeat despite their best performance of the tournament. I feel the anguish of compassion when you are powerless to help. And Sven, looking lost, is carrying all the weight of the defeat on his shoulders. England has a truly gifted generation of football players and this is recognized worldwide. The level of expectation upon them is so high. Sometimes the pressure of that expectation is simply too much. On the day, either side could have won.

How I manage to run the gauntlet back to the car is a blank – a moment when the world went out. Once Johan and Lina join me we sit in stunned silence on the journey back to Baden-Baden. The car is our warm cocoon against the world. A flood of images begins to invade my consciousness. I see Sven's dejected face trying to control the shame of failure. He really believed in his players. Then I see him proud and triumphant as the winner of the Italian League – the Scudetto. We have shared so much together. Slowly, the realization that my time at the centre of the English football world is coming to an end wells up with a new wave of tears. Can it all be over so soon – just like that – on the outcome of a game? I don't think that I am quite ready for this. And through my tears five years of my life are flashing by.

I remember the warm, spontaneous response for me at Highbury after the first scandal had hit the press, with the fans and the players on the pitch applauding, throwing flowers and shouting my name, 'Nancy, Nancy.' The English seem so reserved at first, but once you break the ice they are the kindest people in the world. I see the enduring image of Trevor MacDonald, who took me by surprise at the Independent Television Awards by introducing me on stage as 'the first lady of football'. This may have been television hype, but for an Italian girl in England – this was recognition. Memories, like my beautiful garden at home in Regent's Park, tea at Claridge's, a day at the races, more tea on the lawn of an Oxford college. Then there is the cheeky, chirpy, Cockney, London thing, where everyone cheers you up with a wry comment on current affairs. I blink back the tears again – surprised I still have any tears left. My stream of consciousness is often over-sentimental – at least that remains Italian. Well, I don't have to leave London if I don't want to! We can always buy that flat in Chelsea. I have never lived in just one place. I don't think I will ever truly leave London.

BORN IN THE USA

•

I love to go and I love
To have been, but, best
Of all, I love the intervals
Between arrivals and departures.

NOEL COWARD

WE ITALIANS LOVE TO TRAVEL AND ADVENTURE IS IN our blood. I am proud to say that it was an Italian explorer, Giovanni da Verrazzano, who, in 1524, was the first European to enter what is now known as New York Bay, where he discovered a beautiful harbour and named it Angouleme (later called Manhattan). So, in true Italian style, my father, Francesco Dell'Olio, took to the seas. He grew up in the southern Italian coastal town of Bisceglie in the region of Apulia (Puglia in Italian) – the little bit of Italy that forms the sharp stiletto heel of the 'boot' on a map, where the Adriatic meets with the Ionian Sea. He came from a long line of fishermen and, although his childhood was not privileged or particularly comfortable, he was happy and healthy and able to look after his three younger sisters. However, unlike his father and his grandfather before him, Francesco realized he wanted more than life in a small fishing community could offer him. He sought adventures in faraway places and, as a budding entrepreneur, looked to the New World and the opportunities that it could offer a young man. After the war, aged twenty, he began work as a communications officer on transatlantic shipping between Italy and the United States. However, after a few years this peripatetic life began to pall and the lure of terra firma and the land of opportunity became too strong for him to ignore. He handed in his notice and decided to try his luck in America.

In fact, my father was not the first member of the extended family to have been tempted by the lifestyle America could provide. His uncle and aunt had already emigrated to the USA some years earlier, and now owned a ranch just outside the Californian town of Fresno. Armed only with a scribbled address on a piece of paper, which he had kept carefully in the back of a book, Francesco set off to find his relatives. When he finally arrived, he was welcomed into the family and quickly made new friends within the Italian immigrant community that had settled in the area. Fresno, in California's San Joaquin Valley, was uninhabited until the 1860s but built up a prosperous agricultural industry after the 1880s, when Italian immigration began. With its mild winters and very hot summers, it must have felt like home to the Italians who went there in large numbers in the early 1900s, mostly families from Sicily and, later, veterans of the First World War and political opponents of Mussolini. There was a thriving wine and raisin industry, and extensive wheat and dairy farming on large ranches.

At first, Francesco helped out on the ranch in return for board and lodging. But the farming life was not for him and soon he was restless to be on the move. He had big ideas and couldn't wait to turn them into reality. He also realized that he would need to improve his English and further his education if he wanted to make it in the world of American business. After talking things through with his uncle, he decided to leave the California sunshine and head north-east to the Big Apple – New York City. My father has often said, 'I love America because it gave me a chance in life,' and the decision to move to New York was to change his life in more ways than one.

Francesco loved New York from the moment he arrived. Despite the weather – which can be very cold in winter and unbearably hot in summer – he felt completely at home amongst the Italian community. Italian immigrants had first arrived in New York City in the late nineteenth century to escape unemployment and poverty at home and by 1920 there were almost 400,000 Italians living in the city, mostly around Bleeker Street, Elizabeth Street and Baxter Street – the area that became known as Little Italy. By the mid-1950s, when my father arrived there, the number of Italian families in the area had fallen, but there were still enough for the place to have a comforting familiarity. He made friends easily and quickly settled in, pleased to feel part of a 'family' and participating in the various traditional Italian feast days and celebrations. Although he was keen to take advantage of everything America had to offer, he certainly hadn't forgotten his roots! He has told me about one particular group of artistic New York friends who introduced him to painting and literature – a real eye-opener for the fisherman's son from Apulia. In later life this was to become a passion for him (and for me, too), but for now he was keen to pursue his primary goal – to make his way in business.

My father found rooms in Brooklyn and took on part-time work to help with the cost of his studies. Despite living and working within the Italian community, he made sure he spoke English and mixed with English speakers as much as possible in order to improve his vocabulary and grammar. In fact, he had always been very good at languages at school and he learned quickly. He was soon confident enough to apply to the University of New York to study economics and business, and was accepted. His uncle and aunt agreed to help with his fees and, spurred on by his determination to succeed, he managed to combine his studies with part-time jobs to pay his board and lodging.

After completing his university course, my father set about developing his own business. He had always been interested in the food industry – food is never far from the heart of a true Italian – and had an idea for a chain of old-European-style New York-Italian deli restaurants. What he had in mind was similar to the fast-food ideas that would become popular decades later, so he was well ahead of his time. He started with just one restaurant but it proved so popular that he began to think about expanding. He found financial backers and partners from within the Italian community who could see that he had drive and ambition and wasn't afraid of hard work. Within a few years, that investment was to pay off as the business grew from that single restaurant into an organization with over fifty outlets. In fact, the company even received a medal of achievement from the Mayor of New York City.

While my father was busy developing his business, a young girl called Antonia Saladino was growing up in that same New York-Italian neighbourhood, but their paths were not to cross until 1958. Antonia was born to an Italian-Jewish couple, Fiorello and Edina Saladino. I suspect there is some Arab blood in the family line too, as the name Saladin would imply. Fiorello had been in the US army during the war, and had stayed on after the war had ended, so Antonia was born an American citizen. Her mother was from strong Jewish-American stock. The women of the family in particular tend to live long lives: my grandmother reached the grand old age of a hundred in 2004. Coincidentally, the Saladino family had also emigrated from the region of Apulia, so when the budding entrepreneur Francesco eventually met Antonia, it was as if the call of their native land had drawn them together. When they met, as they have both told me on many occasions, it was love at first sight. They had a whirlwind romance and married just six months after their first meeting. My grand-mother, jokingly, always said that my father married my mother to obtain his US passport. While this may have been a beneficial side-effect of their romance, they are still together some forty-eight years later and, as far as I am aware, have forged a happy relationship through their highs and lows together.

With my father's business going from strength to strength, Francesco and Antonia settled down happily to married life. At first they lived in Brooklyn and, while my father went out to work at his restaurants each day, my mother kept house and did part-time translation work. Of course, Italians love children and it wasn't long before they decided to start a family of their own, so this is where my own story begins.

Following an earlier miscarriage, both my parents were delighted when, after three years of marriage, my mother found she was expecting again. I was born under the star sign of Virgo, making my first grand entrance at the Manhattan Memorial Hospital. In Italian tradition, it is said that a child receives three gifts from his or her parents. First of all, there is the gift of birth itself. The second gift is the place of birth – in my case, New York City. The third gift is the power of a name. Wise women say that destiny is in the name given to a child. However, I was lucky to escape the destiny of the family name my father first chose for me – Annunciata, after his grandmother. Can you imagine the torture I would have endured in the schoolyard in 1960s America? Luckily for me, I had a strong mother who – in true Saladino style – put her foot down. She wanted something more American for her firstborn, with maybe just a taste of Italy. Eventually they settled upon Nancy.

I was the eldest of the four children my parents would eventually have, but for that first year I was their only child. I used to dismiss the idea of birth-order trauma as a myth, or psychobabble, but after much reflection on family relationships I have come to believe that birth order does, in fact, often condition your life. Being born first creates a real feeling of heightened expectation in both the parents and the child, not to mention the anxiety which the parents experience when realizing that this new little life is completely dependent on them – an anxiety which, no doubt, the child picks up too. For a year I had my parents all to myself, and then my brother Jerome came along. They say that when the first sibling arrives, the loss of undivided attention creates a wound from which you never recover. Although I do not remember ever consciously having thought this, I can understand how it could be the case. I have always liked to be the centre of attention, and I am sure this is my way of trying to get back to being the only child who can command undivided love from her two parents. The new addition to the family must have stirred up some jealousy deep within me because Jerome became the target of my frustration at the perceived sense of betrayal by my parents. Apparently, so my grandfather Girolamo (my father's father) told me, I was once discovered in Jerome's bedroom holding a pair of scissors. Jerome was sleeping peacefully, blissfully unaware of any danger. Quite what I was intending to do, I have no idea, and of this event I have no memory. Suffice to say, I must have felt threatened – without any foundation, I must add – and considered Jerome to be a rival. Behind so much negative emotion hides a terrified child who fears abandonment. Thankfully, Jerome survived my childhood jealousy and, I have to say, he is now one of my closest friends, as well as a loving brother and sometime collaborator.

Jerome and I – the two eldest children of the family – have a special bond as we were both born in New York (my younger sister and brother were born later in Italy). So we shared our formative years together. I think to be the firstborn means that you grow up faster, and perhaps there is more pressure on you; no wonder many world leaders and successful business people occupy this primary position in their families. Whatever I did, Jerome would follow not far behind. I became the organizer and Jerome was happy to play along, desperate to keep up with his older sister. Despite my early misgivings about this uninvited usurper, we became inseparable.

A child absorbs the world through the reactions of her parents. Even though I was only a toddler, I could feel their excitement in being alive at this time. I was not yet born at the time of such world-changing events as the Cuban Missile Crisis or the tragic death of the great movie star Marilyn Monroe, but the emotional climate of the 1960s was almost tangible and permeated my child's imagination. Even if I cannot remember the details, I can still feel the nostalgia of shared experience from my parents' stories – and picture the impressions they left – as vividly today as I did then. After all, this was the era of John Glenn, the first American to orbit the earth; the building of the Berlin Wall; the American Civil Rights Movement; and the creative minds of Andy Warhol and the Beatles.

Having spent my very early years in the bosom of the family, the day eventually arrived when I had to go to school. I was four years old when my parents enrolled me in the local kindergarten. My little uniform made me feel very grown up and I had my own satchel for my books and pencils. It was the first time I had experienced any time away from my family and, at first, the prospect was rather daunting. For a start, I had to leave Jerome at home, and I thought of what he and my mother would be doing without me. But I quickly made friends and enjoyed the company of other children. I also liked the sense of achievement: I was good at art and loved sport and the playground games. Every day my mother would collect me from school and I would go home to show her and Jerome what I had done.

When I think back to my early childhood, the images I see are the places I would visit with my mother and Jerome. How clearly I can picture Washington Square and the shops and restaurants of Greenwich Village, holding on tightly to my mother's hand as she pushed my little brother in his pushchair. Just a whiff of my mother's perfume transports me back to the dressing table in my parents' bedroom at our old apartment in Brooklyn Heights, me standing in front of the mirror while she let me try on her necklaces and shoes (the early signs of my later addiction).

I have fewer memories of my father at this time. Like many men building a future for their families, he worked long hours and often came home late after we children had gone to bed. We did, however, get to spend several weeks with him each summer when, as a family, we would travel back to Italy to visit Apulia. I can remember the contrast between the gentle pace of life in the fishing villages dotted along the coast of the Adriatic and the energy of New York, full of people and cars rushing about and buildings towering into the sky. Summers in Italy were about family, the beach and the sea. These were the times when my father could relax and spend time with his wife and children.

Back in New York, business prospered and by the mid-1960s my father's American dream had come true. However, the day-to-day life in New York became routine and often his heart and imagination would lead him back to the land of his birth. Although he had yearned for adventure and a life different from that of his ancestors, he missed his extended Italian family, to whom he had always been very close, and, having lived life to the full in the New World, had begun to feel nostalgic for the old. He would return to Italy more and more often, and success in the American food industry gave him the funds and opportunity for property investment on both sides of the Atlantic. He had been away from Apulia for more than twelve years and the generations he had known as a young man were passing on. In addition, my father, who is a very traditional man, believed his young family would benefit from the slower pace and stability of life in Italy, just as he had had.

Of course, my mother took some persuading. She, after all, was an American girl who would be leaving her friends and family behind. But our summer holidays had given her a taste of Italy and she, too, could see that there was much to be said for the traditional lifestyle. And so it was that we packed up our lives in America and moved, lock, stock and barrel, to the land of my forefathers. My father is now eighty-one, and all these years later still lives in Apulia with my mother. He rarely goes to America now, but he will always remember the precious gift that country gave our family – the gift of freedom. For me, the return to our Italian roots would herald the start of a new chapter in my life and, once again, fate would play its part.

AN AMERICAN GIRL IN APULIA

•

The memories of women are like secret drawers in an antique sewing box. Because women always have secret drawers. Some of them have been closed for so long that they are almost impossible to reopen. Some are littered with the petals of pressed flowers – like the dust of roses; in some you will find the many-coloured yarns entangled with old needles lost within to prick you. The memories of women are like this.

FROM *ALEXIS* BY MARGUERITE YOURCENAR

I WAS JUST FOUR WHEN WE RETURNED TO ITALY, AND the contrast between life in Manhattan and life in Bisceglie, in Apulia, could not have been greater. Although the move back to his homeland had been instigated by my father, it was my mother, Jerome and I who spent most of our time there, whilst my father commuted between New York and our new home. He bought two properties – an apartment in Bisceglie and another in Rome – although initially we spent most of our time in Bisceglie. He also bought some land on the coast just outside Bisceglie and began to construct the villa that was to become our family home, and where my parents still live.

Bisceglie itself is quite a large town, with a population of nearly fifty thousand, but it seemed quiet and laid back after the hustle and bustle of New York. For Jerome and I, used to the densely packed, built-up environment of Manhattan, the open expanse of azure blue sky was so exhilarating, and the light which reflected from the sea along the coastline just north of the town was magnificent. Despite being very young, I do not remember being at all apprehensive about starting afresh in a very different part of the world. I seem to remember thinking it was a rather exciting adventure, which I found liberating. I was always very adaptable and, in retrospect, I put this down to the security of knowing that I was much loved as a child, by my parents and by the many members of our extended family who featured in my early years (I quickly became especially close to my cousin Tina). Both Jerome and I settled easily into our new life. During the week I attended the local elementary school where I made new friends, and at weekends I would spend time by the sea with my parents and Jerome. The beach at Bisceglie is very beautiful – a long strip of golden sand bounded by fields of crops, orchards, gardens and lawns, olive groves and purple oleanders. Beyond, the countryside becomes very rural and it is there that you can discover a reminder of the ancient history of this part of the world. Hidden deep within the olive groves stands a Paleolithic monument, a dolmen – or burial chamber – thousands of years old. This quiet, secret place was my special hideaway, and I would often take myself off there in the summer to read or paint, with only the serenade of cicadas for company.

Within a short time, our new family villa by the sea was ready to move into, and this was to become one of my favourite places. Even now, I like to go back there to visit the family as much as possible and to be reminded of the carefree days of my childhood. There were other changes in our family, too. Two more children were born in Italy: first my sister Fiorella arrived, then, shortly afterwards, my brother Gianfranco. The competition for my parents' attention – and particularly my mother's – was hotting up.

Living by the sea in such a wonderful climate meant that I spent a great deal of my childhood out of doors. Soon after our move to Italy, we had acquired two new canine members of the family – a French poodle, or *barboncino*, Coco, and a German Shepherd called Willie. My mother and I would often take long walks along the ribbon of beach with the dogs, and so began my lifelong love of these faithful friends. Having had many dogs in the family over the years, I consider myself more of a dog lover than a cat person, though, unfortunately, my busy lifestyle now means that it would be unfair for me to have my own dog. My father's favourites were German Shepherds – strong and loyal protectors – but my mother loved her poodles and I, too, acquired a soft spot for them as they are such intelligent animals. I am told that large hunting poodles were the sporting dogs of choice for the French kings and, despite their looks, they should not be underestimated.

The beach was also the place for fun and games, and it was here that I learned to play tennis and volleyball. I remember many happy, sunny afternoons, filled with laughter and shouting, as I played with my siblings and the other children. I was always quite a sporty child, and enjoyed athletics and gym classes.

In fact, I would attribute my health and overcoming rheumatic ailments as a child to my open-air, energetic lifestyle.

When I was not at school or on the beach, I loved to dance. However, my parents were also keen to encourage my musical skills and agreed to ballet lessons only if I also learned to play the piano. Therefore piano lessons were arranged for me at the local conservatoire, a *convento* run by nuns. For a free spirit like me, all the practising of scales and exercises was pure torture. Worst of all was the fact that the piano practice sometimes took place in one of the grand old convent assembly rooms where they stored all the stone statues of the saints. These life-sized figures stood before me, all draped in eerie grey dustcloths, looking – to my childish eyes – like a company of dead souls, an august assembly of heaven gathered round in silent witness of my feeble attempts. I hated every hour I spent there and yearned only to escape. One day, during one of these torturous sessions, I was suffering from a painful throat infection and was feeling particularly low. Growing ever more apprehensive as I stared at the bare feet of all these saints poking out from under their ghostly shrouds, I decided that I had to escape. I got up from the piano and tiptoed over to the old sash window. Looking out, I reasoned that the first-floor window where I stood was probably within jumping distance of the grass outside. It was worth the risk, so I gathered up my courage and – quickly and quietly, so as not to be discovered – slipped the catch and used all my strength to lever up the window and edge out on to the sill. Although it was a long way down and I knew I would land with a bump, it was nothing compared with the horror of endless scales and the fear of being shut up with those ghoulish figures. So I made the jump, rolled with the fall and ran back home to Mama. Having made the break for freedom, there was no way I was going to go back to that convent and, particularly, to face the wrath of the nuns. However, when my mother found out what I had done, she marched me back to class and, to my chagrin, I found myself back again with those dreaded saints. Not to be outdone, I ran away again, but this time the nuns discovered I had gone and went to my home to report me missing. Following this second incident, they agreed to let me have my piano practice in a different room, but the trauma had put me off the instrument for life. I did manage to pass my first accompanied concert exam, but my parents then allowed me to give up the piano and to focus on ballet instead. I still love to watch ballet today and, in many ways, I can see similarities between a game of football and a ballet. Both dancers and football players are extremely fit and agile, and they both require a tremendous sense of control and precision.

I inherited part of my sense of glamour from my mother who was, and still is, a very naturally glamorous woman. Having been born and bred in America, she was perhaps more modern, ambitious and open-minded in her approach to life than the Italian mothers of my friends. She always stood out from the other parents at the school gate and I was very proud of her.

My parents were also quietly proud of us, although they certainly didn't approve of boasting of their children's achievements. This often led me to show off in front of them and, as I have said before, I did like to be the centre of attention. As a result, I was always happy to stand up in class to read or recite poems, and every year I would find myself on stage acting in the school play and taking part in my ballet school's annual performance. This was the origin of my fascination with the world of acting and my sense of the theatrical. I have a taste for the flamboyant and, back then, would spend hours dressing up, usually in my grandmother's clothes, shuffling along on too-high heels and experimenting with hair and make-up.

While my mother took care of most of the parenting, my father continued to be busy with his interests. He was lucky enough to be able to escape the pressure of having to work for a living while still in his early forties, but he continued to make investments in both Europe and the United States, so he still travelled frequently. As a result, he never really retired and continued to manage operations. Although he was absent for what seemed large parts of my early life, I never experienced his being away as traumatic. It was what I was used to and seemed perfectly normal to me. So strong is the established patriarchal presence in most traditional Italian families that, like the sun in the sky, you don't have to be able to touch it in order to feel the heat or see the light. And when he returned from his business tours, he would arrive laden with presents, which made him very popular with us children.

During the school holidays my parents loved nothing more than to pack us all into the family car and go touring. At first we would mainly travel around Apulia and the surrounding provinces, where my father introduced us to the places he had known as a child. Later we travelled further afield to visit all the great classical cities of Italy.

Apulia is a long, narrow peninsula of rolling plains and hills. The Adriatic Sea forms the eastern border, with the Ionian Sea, the Strait of Otranto and the Gulf of Taranto to the south. It has always been a gate to and from the east and, as such, has suffered many conquests. Most of its foreign lords were never resident, but one exception was the fascinating Frederick II, the thirteenth-century Holy Roman Emperor who was the last of the Hohenstaufen line. He left behind the many castles, vineyards and olive groves that give the region its character. I loved the historic atmosphere and the presence of the past, which contrasted markedly with our previous surroundings in New York. Apulia features a fusion of architectural styles, from Romanesque to Moorish, and I think this must have led to my later interest in house design and property in general. Indeed, these early excursions must have had more of an influence on us than I realized at the time, since I later developed many properties of my own and my brother, Jerome, became an architect.

All along the Adriatic coast are dozens of small *trattorie* – or local restaurants – serving freshly caught fish in the Pugliese style, usually simply marinated and grilled or sometimes with a fresh tomato sauce. We would often stop at one of these inns for lunch to enjoy the super-fresh seafood with wonderful vegetables, and the delicious sun-ripened fruit of the region – plums, peaches, apricots and cherries. Although we had eaten traditional Italian dishes in New York, I had never before tasted food so fresh and with that intensity of flavour you get only from food grown and produced locally. I know I was spoiled from an early age, but it made me appreciate really good food, and I have always enjoyed eating a healthy diet. The only aspect of the Italian diet that my American heritage has never really understood is their habit of eating all types of feathered creatures.

My father's favourite monument to visit on our travels was the thirteenth-century Castel del Monte just south of Andria. This was Frederick II's favourite hunting lodge and it is quite unique: an octagonal Gothic castle, with eight towers and eight trapezoidal rooms on each floor. I think my father's fascination with history rubbed off on me and these family tours always felt like an immersion in living time, with all three dimensions of the past, present and future layered in, like parallel themes within a story. I am not sure that I believe in reincarnation, but the sense of having lived before is often like a sliding door. If ever I have had this feeling of living in a past life, the Castel del Monte and the era of Emperor Frederick II have always evoked it. The castle, sited on a peak, dominates the entire region and the valley outside

Andria, forming a single point of orientation. You can see it from almost everywhere – from the harbours and beaches, from out at sea as far away as the Gulf of Manfredo, from the Murgian highlands and from the fields and the forest. Even the tall buildings of modern cities are overarched. The castle is steeped in arcane symbolic meaning and brings together all the diverse cultural elements of the time – the location, the mathematical and astronomical precision of the design, and the perfectly regular shape. The octagonal plan – repeating the number eight – has obvious esoteric significance and blends the elements of Byzantine classical antiquity, the Islamic orient and the northern European Gothic.

Emperor Frederick II is one of my great heroes, as he presided over a unique flowering of culture in southern Italy which was a precursor to the Renaissance. As a patron of the Sicilian school of poetry, his royal court gave birth to a literary form of the Italo-Romance language, Sicilian; the school and the poetry were well known to Dante and influenced the literary form of what was to become modern Italian. Rather than persecuting the Saracens of Sicily, Frederick allowed them to settle on the mainland and build mosques. His tolerance of Islam earned him a place in the sixth circle of Dante's Inferno, heretic Hell. Tolerance of other people's beliefs and ways of life has always been important to me and I think the influence of Frederick II was an early trigger in this way of thinking.

There is no doubt that my interest in the Middle East and

the principles of sovereignty and law may be traced to my youthful imaginings of the court of imperial Sicily. The castle is so wonderfully preserved that, looking at it, you can almost be transported back to the period of the Crusades. Even in that world, Frederick was very different. Unlike the Crusaders who sacked the sacred city of Jerusalem and slaughtered its inhabitants, Frederick camped his army outside and began to negotiate with the Ayyubid Sultan of Egypt. Within five months the city was surrendered to him and he was able to declare himself King of Jerusalem. When the patriarch of Jerusalem refused to crown him, Frederick placed the crown upon his own head. His reign in Jerusalem was, however, shortlived and by 1244 he had lost the city again to a new Muslim offensive. One of my favourite films is Ridley Scott's *Kingdom of Heaven*, which portrays the rich cultural cross-fertilization of this period so wonderfully.

Another place we would often visit was Trani, where the cathedral overlooks the water and the fishing harbour, and the caverns of Castellana Grotte with their spectacular stalagmites and stalactites. Then we would head south into Apulia's most fairy-tale region, the land of the *trulli*. These cylindrical huts, made without mortar and topped with gnome-like conical grey stone roofs, look as if they have come straight out of the Shire in the films of Tolkein's *Lord of the Rings*. Magical whitewashed buildings, which look like beehives from a distance, they date from the seventeenth century and are often marked with hex symbols to ward off evil spirits.

So this was the landscape and the culture that grounded my Italian and European identity, as distinct from my earlier American identity. I hope this journey through some of the memories of my Italian girlhood has illustrated the influences that shaped the woman I was to become. Although home was in Italy, I continued to spend time in New York, visiting during the summer holidays, and feel that the schizophrenia of dividing my life between the new world of America and the old world of Europe has been the defining force in my life.

I was never a girl for dolls unless they came as presents. Even then it was to dress them up as fashion clothes horses or doctors and nurses; I never thought to play mum or happy families with them. There was never enough life in these inanimate playthings; I preferred to play with living, breathing people – my siblings or my friends.

My first experience of death was that of the elder daughter of close family friends from New York, who also moved back to Italy around the same time that we did. Although they lived quite far away, we occasionally met up and I played with the younger daughter, who was a similar age to me. Sadly, her elder sister suffered from a rare blood disease and this led to her tragic early death at just eighteen. I don't remember even being aware that she was ill. One moment she was alive, and the next she was dead. I think the thing that struck me was the finality of the loss: your place in time is at an end. I will never forget the sadness of seeing her laid out in her coffin. She looked like an angel, dressed in her white gown. I could not understand how someone so beautiful and so young could be dead. Even now, as I write, my eyes fill with tears and I think of the words of the poet John Keats: 'A thing of beauty is a joy for ever'. Unfortunately, we lost touch with the family, but I heard that a few years later the younger sister also died from the same disease. I remember her so vividly from when we were teenagers together, both bursting with life.

It was shortly after this time that my parents thought it would be beneficial to broaden our horizons beyond the little town of Bisceglie. We had an apartment in Rome and it was decided that we would move there during the week and that I would go to the American International School in the city. Despite having adapted well to the Italian way of life, my mother was still an American at heart and she was keen for me to have an international perspective. I don't have many memories of this period, perhaps as a result of the amnesia I suffered after the accident I had aged twenty-one, which I will discuss in detail in the next chapter. My recollections of my school years are confused and dreamlike. I know I liked to do my own thing and never followed the crowd like some of the other girls. Perhaps that made me a bit of a loner, but I certainly never felt lonely. Of course, I did have friends – some very good ones, with whom I am still in touch today. My particular friends were Sylvia and Cinzia and we were, I suppose, just a normal group of girls, but the bond we created was lasting. Even though we are often separated by many miles – and sometimes a year will go by without a chance to see each other – we have a connection and can pick up where we left off.

As a young girl, I wasn't particularly interested in boys either – perhaps because I had two brothers! I didn't even have a proper boyfriend until I was eighteen, although I do remember having a juvenile crush on a little friend of Jerome. Younger men have never been my preference but, on this occasion, I think I was infatuated. Of course it was all in my mind and, looking back, the poor boy must have been completely bemused by this unwanted attention from his friend's elder sister.

After a short while in Rome, we decided to move back to Bisceglie. Perhaps, having got used to the Italian way of schooling, I didn't flourish at the American International School, and so I went back into the Italian system. On our return to Apulia, I was enrolled at a *liceo* and it was there that I spent the rest of my secondary education.

On the whole, my early childhood was a very happy one. Although I was always curious and quite independent, this was not a problem whilst I was still young enough to be under my mother's thumb and lacked the freedom to express my will. However, as I entered my teenage years and began to develop my personality, I am the first to admit that life became more difficult – for me and, as I am sure they would testify, for my parents. I felt like I had fallen between two stools – neither fish nor fowl (or neither fish nor meat, as we would say in Italian). On the one hand I was no longer a child, but neither was I a woman. I felt as if I wanted to fast-forward those awkward years of puberty and get it all over and done with. Like my father, I was strong-minded and this led to a particularly tempestuous relationship with my mother at this time. My father, who was still shuttling back and forth between Italy and America, was not in my firing line so often and escaped much of what my mother had to put up with. Looking back, I think I was testing her love for me. She had given her life to looking after her children and, whilst she was never resentful of me or my sister and brothers, maybe I sensed a feeling of personal unfulfilment in her. Perhaps for her I was born too early, and parenthood curtailed her ability to have her own career or to develop her own interests. I think many ambitious women of her generation felt the same way; it was more difficult for women then to 'have it all'. Most children believe that life revolves around them, and I was no exception. That your parents – in my case, my mother in particular – might have a life of their own, in their own right, is difficult to understand and accept. It wasn't until I was older that I could see how trying my behaviour might have been.

My parents felt I was growing up too fast and disapproved of my keeping company with the slightly older set I moved with. I had always looked for approval from older people, so perhaps that explains my attraction to a more mature crowd and the companionship of older souls. One relationship in particular tried both my parents to breaking point. I had grown close to a woman in her forties who was breaking up with her husband and family of three children to live with a new love. Her husband was well respected within the community and was a pillar of the establishment. I was fascinated by her and the glamour she exuded – she worked in fashion and was always immaculately turned out. I felt a great affinity for this woman that no amount of parental disapproval could change. Her behaviour was universally frowned upon, but I admired her because she had made a choice to be true to herself in the full knowledge of the pain she would cause to herself and to those she loved. I believed that she showed great courage – the courage to love in the full knowledge of the high price that must be paid. The fact that she was prepared to give up everything for love fascinated me in my early years of naive romantic aspiration.

As I say, I had always felt older than my years and couldn't wait to be eighteen. When, at last, I reached that magical age, the prospect of going to law school at the University of Bari, one of Italy's finest, was electrifying. This was the beginning of the journey I had been longing for since childhood. My sense of hunger for real experience was overwhelming. For youth in waiting for adulthood, time goes by so slowly. I had not yet learned to be present in the moment. Looking back down the long road of my time, I can understand the maxim of George Bernard Shaw, that 'youth is wasted on the young'. However, I think that, in becoming an adult, we must try to maintain our 'inner child'. A sense of wonder keeps us young, adaptable and creative.

Born under the sign of Virgo, I have an analytical mind and an eye for detail. I had always been interested in the law and I dreamed of studying law and jurisprudence, the philosophy that underpins the practice of law, and eventually joining the legal profession. I admired the generation of young, smart and stylish women lawyers that was emerging within the profession. The study of law would also give me a practical direction to balance my more mystical leanings and my love of poetry. Of course, there was the added bonus that the young men in the law faculty were both intelligent and handsome. What more could a young girl want!

My first real love, however, was not a lawyer. A successful businessman, he was from an old and aristocratic Italian family and just fell passionately in love with me. After nineteen summers, and all of that awakening womanhood, it is easy to think you are in love with someone who flatters you by falling in love with you. He was very sweet, charming and caring, but I was not ready for the intensity of a relationship. I wanted to find a way of extricating myself from the situation, but without hurting the man. So I took myself off for the rest of the summer – to Paris.

My friend Patrizia, whom I met in my first year at university, had gone to study in Paris and loved to beguile me with romantic stories of that fabulous city. My mother was also encouraging me to broaden my talents. I had always loved cooking and, as a fabulous cook herself, she had taught me many of her favourite dishes. I was, I thought justifiably, proud of my skill and for my eighteenth birthday I threw a large and extravagant dinner party at my parents' house by the sea. It became something of a tradition – I was quite famous among my circle for these birthday dinners. Now a Cordon Bleu summer school in Paris seemed like a wonderful opportunity to hone my traditional skills. What girl would turn down the chance of a long summer in Paris, the chance to learn about *dolci* – desserts – and how to plan and prepare for dinner parties? To my mind, the dinner party was the next best thing to a salon and I had always imagined myself as the smart society hostess. However, the Cordon Bleu course cooked up a recipe for rebellion which I am sure my parents had not anticipated. This was my first real taste of freedom – no parents and no teachers or tutors to keep an eye on me or tell me what to do. Despite her exciting stories of Parisian adventure, what Patrizia had failed to tell me was that she had been staying in a convent with the nuns. Consequently, she had a curfew and had to be back early each evening. I was having none of that and would stay out all night, visiting clubs and parties, and really letting my hair down. Needless to say, my parents found out and insisted I come home immediately. But, once free, the sweet bird of youth does not want to return to its cage.

After my hedonistic summer in Paris, I went back to university and settled again into work and my social life. Throughout my adult life, many of the men in my circle of friends have been gay and I have always enjoyed the friendship and company of the more sensitive man. But a man for me – in a romantic sense – must be a man. The most attractive alpha male is not afraid of his feminine side – just as a woman must embrace the masculine within her. I gained great comfort in interpreting myself to myself by reading the greats in classics and philosophy. I think the insights Freud uncovered a hundred years ago have yet to be adequately integrated into a modern theory of human nature. My feeling is that, despite some errors natural to his time, his core insight into the unconscious ground of human behaviour remains acute. This is not an intellectual subjugation of the animal nature. We swim in an invisible world of cerebral processing that the conscious mind is too slow to grasp. It is only our intuitive nature – the feminine intelligence called Sophia, or wisdom – that can lead us out of the labyrinth of our conditioning.

Most red-blooded girls who attend university end up falling in love with the proverbial professor and I was no exception. In my case, it wasn't just one. The first was a young law professor in his early forties with a powerful reputation. We had the usual student–teacher grand passion. I can't exactly remember now if I seduced him or if he seduced me. Suffice to say that the infatuation was mutual. Thus, I was initiated to mature romances, breaking unwritten rules, and the excitement of secrecy heightened every emotion. A short while later, I found myself falling into a passionate interaction of minds – it was the intellect that drew me, rather than the body – of another member of the faculty, who was going through marital problems. He introduced me to the great classics and taught me how to read them. Fortunately, my parents were not really aware of my pseudo-bohemian love life.

I knew from an early age that my life would not be conventional or ordinary. I never experienced that female biological imperative to get married and have babies that, I know, some girls do. I had seen how giving birth and raising a family can so completely monopolize a woman's attention that she has no time left for herself. So intent was I on the exploration of my own individuality that I had no wish to sacrifice my freedom in order to have children and a family of my own. Of course, I fell in and out of love a few times, as young girls always do, but I was more in love with the idea of being in love, and the excitement of being – in the words of the old cliché – footloose and fancy free. I enjoyed the feeling of being noticed and desired, and playing the Italian game of 'I was looking back, to see if he was looking back, to see if I was looking back at him'. I was too young and too naive to understand what I was doing.

Suffering is often life's way of making you wake up and face your responsibilities. It is that feeling that, when everything seems just too good to be true, fortune exacts a payback. I was just twenty-one, spending the summer holidays with my parents at our villa and about to get that wake-up call. If I think hard, I can take myself back to the moments before my world went blank.

COMA

●

The most beautiful thing we can experience is the mysterious.
It is the source of all true art and science.

ALBERT EINSTEIN

IV IT WAS A SATURDAY, EARLY EVENING, WHEN MY WORLD was changed for ever. It had been an ordinary day, just like any other Saturday. I was just about to leave for a university term in New York to gain extra credits, so I had spent it with my family and out doing a bit of shopping. Looking back, there were no ominous signs and nothing had happened to alert me to the black cloud on the horizon. I was looking forward to an evening out with my friends and had spent a couple of hours bathing, doing my hair and putting on my make-up, as girls do. I had chosen a white dress to show off my summer tan and a pair of pretty sandals – a recent purchase during a trip to Rome. As I said goodbye to my parents, I – and they – could not have imagined that I was about to have my first brush with death.

The front door of my parents' villa opened directly on to the village high street. I was in a happy mood and full of anticipation for the evening ahead. I greeted my friends, Patrizia and Alfredo, who had called for me, and went to get into the driver's seat of my car. As I opened the door I turned to look behind me. I can only remember the panic and shock of seeing a white car hurtling towards me on the wrong side of the road. It was too close for me to move out of its way and, within a split second, it had hit me, knocking me into the car door and down to the ground. I have no memory of the actual impact or whether I felt any pain – nothing, until I came round in the intensive-care unit of the hospital in Bari. Apparently, the car had been travelling at nearly 70 m.p.h. and knocked me 20 metres down the road from the initial impact. My friends, who had witnessed the accident, were shocked and afraid that I might be dead. Alfredo told me that he rushed up to me, picked me up and moved me away from the road. Patrizia had gone straight to my parents' villa and called an ambulance. The doctors told me later that the ambulance crew who had attended me had been very distressed at seeing such a young girl lying crumpled, unconscious and bleeding. One of them had described me as 'like the dying robin, *pettirosso*, in the snow' in my bloodstained white dress.

I had been knocked unconscious and my physical injuries were substantial. I had been pushed against the frame of my car door, which had cut into my face causing the right side to be badly damaged. My right cheek was mostly ripped off and I lost all sensitivity in my right eye and my lips. I had also broken my pelvis and my left arm and leg. It was a miracle that I had survived, but I had spent a week in a coma.

The experience of such a horrific accident has made me live for the moment, for, like that white Fiat, we never know what is just around the corner. To come to the realization that you are alive requires a conscious moment. I had many such moments during the period of recovery. Of course, a major accident like this is bound to make a person question life, fate and death, and for some people such a turning point never comes; but I now know that there is nothing like the nearness of death to awaken our consciousness of life.

My fascination with the mystery of consciousness and the conscious mind can, I am sure, be traced back directly to my accident and the suffocating experience of coma. Sometimes, when I hear of a brain-dead accident victim, or the living nightmare of the condition that is described in mercilessly clinical language as a 'persistent vegetative state', I get claustrophobia or a feeling of panic, as if drowning in an abyss. There is a world of difference between a dreamer and a mind that is completely blank. When you dream you may not remember, but you do not lose yourself or stop being a conscious subject. This is the most terrifying experience known to man – the sense of dying.

I sometimes imagine myself in this deep and dreamless void, my body and brain operating at a minimum level. The incessant brain chatter has ceased and I am almost in a state of suspended animation. The fear of this state of nothingness is still with me – the sense of terror sometimes returns when I am overtired or disorientated by travel.

At some stage, the dreams began again. I could feel myself rising up, like a dolphin from the deep ocean, as if ascending through different spheres towards the light. I have memories of the doctors standing over me and a sense of temperature and touch returning. My body felt as if it was wrapped up, swaddled in sheets, and I was oddly pain-free, no doubt from the cocktail of drugs that also confused my mind. I have a conviction that, during the 'lost days', I discovered a door inside myself which opened into a different world within – a spiritual world that is too extraordinary and incomprehensible to describe. All I know is that, despite the bad taste in my mouth and the clinical hospital smells, I awoke from my coma with a feeling of elation. As I struggled to open my eyes and make sense of the world, I felt as if I had been born again. The girl I had been before the accident had gone for ever. In her place was a young woman – battle-scarred and broken, but determined to put herself back together and make the most of what life had to offer.

After coming out of the coma, I spent many weeks in hospital in Bari, enduring several operations to mend my broken limbs and reconstruct my face. It was a slow and painful process, but I was over the worst and thankful to be alive.

After the initial period in Bari, I went to a special medical clinic in Tuscany to continue my convalescence and to have more reconstructive microsurgery to my face. Initially I had a huge scar, which, thankfully, has faded over the years. In fact, I think my friends and family were more concerned about the potential disfigurement than I was at the time. I think I just felt lucky that the damage wasn't a lot worse. The experience has, however, put me off facial surgery and I don't think I would ever willingly put myself through some of the cosmetic procedures that women go through today.

The enforced rest gave me time out from my normal life to read, think and consider my future. I loved to listen to music whilst I was reading, and took time to exercise and re-educate my body. Once my bones had mended, I needed lots of physiotherapy just to be able to stand and walk again. I think my passion for health and fitness may stem from this period of incapacity. I did not like the feeling of helpless dependency or of being an invalid. This is why we must have the utmost consideration for those who are disabled or incapacitated in some way.

A near-death experience is life-changing at such a young age. The period of recovery gave me time to think and turned my trauma into a positive belief that there is more to life and the universe than the limited preconceptions of human knowledge. Shakespeare said it all in the words of Hamlet: 'There are more things in heaven and earth, Horatio, than are dreamt of in your philosophy.' It was during this time that I went through my 'spiritual' stage and read many esoteric philosophy books and reimmersed myself in the classics of

European literature I had been introduced to at the *liceo*. Among them were the *Iliad*, Dante and the Italian classical poets, as well as Shakespeare and the Romantic poets – Keats, Shelley and the troubled English hero, Lord Byron. I was fascinated by their enchantment with Rome, nature and classical romance. The origin of the Romantic spirit goes back beyond the classical traditions of Greece and Rome to the ancient mysteries. As I read the works of the poets, I could relate my experience of being in a coma to the depth of mystery they strove to describe and induce through their work. I have never forgotten the comfort of reading the words of these independent minds; they seemed to share with me the terror and the redemption of this great encounter with the unknown. The Romantics guide us to a much richer existence than that of mere intellect. I had learned a vital lesson: in finding myself helpless, I had no alternative but to trust in my deepest nature. I think the secret of my positive inner disposition now is surrender to that trust.

The fear of sliding between two worlds lingered. I loved to hear the everyday sounds of life around me; it gave me comfort to know that everything was 'normal'. In fact, I craved company and noise, rather than peace and quiet. The nights could be like an ocean to cross, and sleeping on my own brought back the shadow of the void. I still do not like to sleep alone; and the bed is always too big without the presence of my man.

When I was ready to leave the clinic, I returned home to

Apulia and spent the next few weeks being looked after by my parents. This period was something of a rapprochement for us – the fact that we had come so close to losing each other, and an acknowledgement of what was really important in life, brought us closer together. Of course, that love and respect had always been there; at some point, life and egos had just got in the way of the parent–child bond. I had grown up, and they had nearly lost me; needless to say, all was forgiven.

Ever since the accident, I have had a fear of cars that has put me off driving, and I have contempt for all people who drive irresponsibly and without what the English term 'due care and attention'. A car is a lethal weapon and I believe that the full rigour of the law should be applied to those who recklessly abuse their licence to drive. Ultimately, I know I was fortunate not to have been more seriously hurt or permanently damaged, and the facial injuries were more character-giving than disfiguring. The real beauty we see in a human face is a gift from years of life. A girl of twenty may be pretty or good-looking, but true inner beauty is a work of art that the experience of living gives to our features. I think Orwell was right in saying that 'by fifty we all have the face we deserve'. I can't wait to see it.

During my time of recovery and the extended physio-therapy sessions, I developed a bit of an addiction to massage. I think it must be something I inherited from my Roman ancestors – a love of thermal baths and pampering. Or maybe I just have a passion for life's little luxuries! Joking aside, I found then and now that a good massage is a great way to ease all those aches and pains; at least I can use the accident as an excuse to indulge myself. I would happily travel the world over in search of a good spa – I was lucky that there were some very good ones on my doorstep.

After my extended convalescence period, I prepared to return to university and take up my studies again. I had missed almost a year of the course and was now well behind my contemporaries. However, I found it remarkably easy to pick up where I had left off. Although I had lost some memories, there was nothing of any major consequence. As far as my love life was concerned, it seemed that the accident ultimately resulted in spicing it up. There was one particular professor to whom I was especially attracted. On my first morning in his class, I made a rather grand and slow entrance on my crutches, crossing the room to take up a seat right in front of him. I think he was rather beguiled by this injured, fragile girl and it brought out all his protective instincts. He couldn't take his eyes off me throughout the class and I knew he was intrigued. At the end of his lesson, all the other, able-bodied students rushed off, eager to get to their next appointments. I, on the other hand, couldn't rush anywhere, which was rather fortuitous, as it gave the professor and I a chance to strike up a conversation. Throughout the course we spent hours in intense academic discussion, but it wasn't until after the exams that he asked me for a date. I enjoyed the romance and it lasted a few months.

The remainder of my time at university held fewer excitements. There was a great deal of studying and a lot of exams, which I passed, graduating with the highest honours. The only question which now remained was where to specialize after graduation. I had no really clear direction and there was no family tradition to follow. The study of law gives you a general background which is fine for business, but if you actually want to join the legal profession, you have to find employment at a law firm and specialize in one area or another. Having read a lot of books on philosophy and psychology, I had a real interest in criminal law and the psychological aspects of these cases. So my preferred path would have been to become a criminal lawyer but, in Italy, this was still a difficult route for a woman. After seeking advice from my tutors and, in particular, my father, I was steered towards property law and soon afterwards was offered an internship with an international law firm in Rome.

THE AVOCATESSA

●

*Once you have flown you will walk the
earth with your eyes turned skywards;
for there you have been, and there
you long to return.*

LEONARDO DA VINCI

ONE OF THE MANY BENEFITS OF TAKING UP A BUSY NEW job in Rome was that it took me away from my old life and the scene of my accident. Memories of being struck by the car still coloured my mind every time I stepped out of the front door of our house in Apulia. Although I would miss my family, there was, to my mind, an obvious need to move away from my childhood home and spread my wings. And what better destination for a fledgling legal eagle than Rome, the city of the imperial eagle itself? The chance of an internship to study international commercial law at a top law firm – Studio Lupoi – in the capital was just what I needed and so I jumped at the opportunity. I packed my bags with all the enthusiasm of youth starting out on a new adventure. Although I had spent a little time in Rome during my teenage years, this would be the first time I would be there on my own terms and free to follow my destiny. As I took to my new life with zeal, the recurrent spectre of the car crash slowly slipped into my long-term memory and I was able to look forward to the challenges ahead of me.

Arriving in Rome is like taking a bath in history. There are few cities in the world that can be classified as living museums in the way that Rome can. You have only to think of that ever-present reminder of the past, the catacombs, with its layers of ancestors packed densely beneath your feet. There, generations of Romans are compressed like coal, built upon and ossified like coral, to form the organic foundations of the Eternal City. I loved to wander around Rome and its museums, just drinking in its ancient splendour. My new-found freedom to explore the city at my leisure made me feel like Audrey Hepburn in *Roman Holiday*. Marianne Faithfull sings about Lucy Jordan 'riding through Paris in a sports car with the warm wind in her hair'. I know what she felt like – but my sports car was in Rome.

Taking up my internship with an old and established top-flight law firm was a daunting prospect. The distinguished senior partners had a formidable reputation and first-term nerves were something that even the law school of Bari had not prepared me for. The practice provided a full range of legal services, both contentious and non-contentious. The civil practice dealt with private clients living and working in Italy, and the business and commercial practice with corporations and business organizations overseas. Rome, as the capital of the Italian Republic, is the seat of all public and administrative institutions, and of the superior jurisdictions and authorities. Understanding how the system worked, in practice, was essential to me after law school in Apulia. The Italian state is still highly centralized, despite the introduction of regional governments. The country's legal processes are based on the Roman system, and a constitutional court, established after the Second World War, determines and upholds the law.

As I watched the *comédie humaine* of day-to-day life within the Roman legal profession, I began to admire the way the up-and-coming women lawyers dressed. They had developed their own style of 'legal chic', managing to combine power-dressing with feminine elegance. The unwritten dress code of the law permits only variations of smart suits on a grey-black-blue theme, but this served only to enhance their professional status in my eyes. I had been used to the student 'uniform' of jeans and radical statement-dressing, so this requirement to dress in a businesslike manner took some adjusting to at first. I soon acquired the wardrobe to go with my new position in life, but that didn't stop me from expressing my wilder side in the evenings or at events, when I cultivated the exotic and theatrical as a pleasing contrast to my professional attire.

As I became more involved in the law, I began to consider why justice was so important to me. I cannot bear injustice, or the denial of justice, in any form. My father, in particular, had always impressed upon me the need for fairness and equality within a set of rules or boundaries. He always explained the rules of the family, but gave us the freedom to make choices within those rules. There is always rivalry within families, between children, just as there is in the wider world, and there needs to be a set of rules that everyone can understand in order for there to be a level playing field. I think that giving the reasons behind rules is as important within families as it is within the law of the land. It is hard to justify rules without a reasonable explanation, and to gain trust and obedience without the knowledge that justice within the rules will be applied impartially. This is really the grounds of natural justice that underpins most of the theories of human rights. Having grown up in a family of four children, I can understand how parental justice, in terms of reward and punishment, is inextricably linked with the need for love. I believe that so much dysfunctional behaviour can be traced to the breakdown of the traditional family within society.

There is always a hierarchy of status being played out in the dominant and subordinate roles of the individuals that comprise a business, and this is just as true in law firms – if not more so – as in any other company. This pecking order – or 'court behaviour', as I like to call it – is aimed at self-promotion, whether the people involved are aware of it or not. As a junior employee, I was fairly low down the pecking order and one of my first jobs was to reorganize the computer systems. The professor I was working with – one of my early mentors – decided that I might benefit from an information and communications technology course in Milan. So, although I had just found my feet and was settling in to a new apartment in Rome, I found myself on the move once again. I had never lived in Milan before, but was rather excited by the prospect of spending six months in the fashion capital of Italy. The computer course was not very stimulating, but the opportunities to shop were limited only by my disposable income. I may not have felt that my legal prospects were enhanced by this interlude in Milan, but my wardrobe certainly was, and I returned to Rome eager to take the next steps in my budding career.

The first few months back in Rome were exceptionally busy and I had little time for anything other than working in the practice and managing clients, and studying during the evenings and weekends for additional qualifications. I may have been a single girl who was not short of male attention, but I didn't have the time or the inclination for a steady relationship. I was quite ambitious but, even without all the work, it would have been difficult to take a break and let my hair down in Rome. Although less so than other Italian cities, Roman society can be traditional and intense, and you are still expected to conform to certain standards of behaviour. Conforming has never been my strong point – I always rebel against any type of social or cultural conditioning – but I had to grit my teeth and get on with it in order to make my way. I had to learn to play the game, both in my professional and in my private life, so my occasional trips to America provided me with a welcome break from this high-pressure existence. I usually took a vacation to New York in December and I loved the contrasts between life in America and in Italy. Having spent my teenage years in Italy, I was more aware of the expectation to conform to Italian stereotypes than to American ones. New York, having such a diverse and multi-cultural population, is a much more accepting society, particularly for those who don't fit the norm. I especially enjoyed the sense of freedom this environment fostered. In New York I could relax, I blended in and could be invisible – it was a great place to just be me for a few weeks.

On a sunny day, Rome is like a succession of stage sets complete with sound effects. The peal of bells, the stutter of Vespa scooters, the shouts of market vendors and street traders, along with the aroma of coffee, dishes clattering on a sidewalk café – all come together to create an almost movie-like illusion of *la dolce vita,* even though that era is long gone. You almost expect to see Fellini's director's chair and hear a cry of 'Lights, camera and action!' Apart from the late addition of Mussolini's imperial boulevards, built in the 1930s, little has changed: Rome escaped much of the nineteenth-century puff so common to most European cities. There is an informality about the blending of the old and the new that gives the city a sense of intimacy that charms visitors. The street lighting is deliberately muted and light pollution is kept to a minimum. This means that on romantic evenings lovers can still see the stars. In my twenties I took all this for granted, but every time I return memories of youth flood back and I realize how much Rome has become a part of me.

At that time, though, I was keen to travel and experience life in other parts of Europe. My legal practice initially offered me the opportunity of a short course in London but, when the chance to study European law in Brussels, the administrative capital of the European Union, was offered as an alternative, I chose to go to there instead. I never dreamed that my own destiny would one day bring me to England. I have always felt a strong connection with the country; I had travelled there on holiday a few times and loved the English countryside. Later, my sister, Fiorella, would move to England more or less permanently. She is an academic at Cambridge, specializing in European citizenship, and a published author. Her daughter, my little niece, was born in England. I had always felt drawn to English poetry. I was also aware of the affinity English people seem to feel for Rome, illustrated by the story of the ailing Romantic poet John Keats, who enjoyed a brief Indian summer of renewal when he came to Rome, knowing he was going to die. Over four thousand people of every nationality are buried in Rome's Protestant cemetery, but the majority of them are English.

After my time in Brussels, I returned again to Rome and the familiar routine of working and studying. My professional and social world was populated with an older crowd of corporate lawyers and businessmen and women, and, when we were not working, we would spend time together in the bars and restaurants of Rome, or entertaining at home. There were many opportunities for romance but, although I flirted with some intent, there was never anyone I was seriously interested in. Many of my male colleagues were already married and the last thing I wanted was the complication of falling in love with a married man. After my experiences at university, I was uncomfortable with the deceit and subterfuge that goes with clandestine relationships. However, I was aware that many of my colleagues were involved in romantic liaisons, privately if not publicly. In the legal world, just as in politics or the entertainment industry, power and passion go together. When the chemistry is firing and the dull routine is electrified with the frisson of a dangerous liaison, lovers are like moths to a flame. The desire is all-consuming, overturning convention, better judgement and common sense. Too often I saw how destructive these relationships could be, and then I would be there for my friends to help pick up the pieces when things went wrong. That wasn't for me. If I was going to have a relationship, I wanted a man fresh and unencumbered.

As my legal career progressed and client-driven activities between Italy and the United States called for me to travel to New York more frequently, the senior partners decided to offer me the chance to continue my postgraduate studies and take up my Masters Degree at New York University. I was exhilarated by the prospect of returning to America, not just to visit but to take up residence again and rediscover my childhood self twenty years on. New York in the 1980s was a European girl's dream and I could not wait to be let loose on

the shops on 5th Avenue in a city booming with all that Wall
Street optimism. My traveller's life has taught me to deal with
the insecurity of moving to new places – wherever I lay my
hat, that's my home. With my wardrobe and my life packed in
my bags, I felt it was time for a new start.

In the mid-eighties New York was the 'Big Apple', and a
boom city in a boom era. I arrived on a high and indulged my
intellectual nostalgia for the era of the Beat Poets, Allen
Ginsberg, Gregory Corso and Jack Kerouac, from the
advantageous perspective of a city that had been going
through a renaissance. The streets had become progressively
safer for hanging out on. The emergence of New Wave music,
hip-hop, new painting and graffiti gave me a sense of being at
the cutting edge. My postgraduate studies at the university
and student activities gave me the chance of an offbeat
lifestyle, and my time in the legal practice working with our
business clients gave me an alternative persona with an Upper
East façade. As part of my work with international Italian-
American corporations, I was also able to experience the 1980s
real-estate bubble at first hand.

There was a big international community in New York and
I made a lot of friends from all walks of life. I loved the
cultural diversity of the city, which is reflected in the large
number of official holidays. The local Italian network hooked
me up with a group of resident Italian correspondents. They
introduced me to a big circle of friends, most of whom were
foreign journalists. In those days of loft parties and easy living,

we made friends from all over: French, Israeli and, of course, English. New York in the 1980s was home to an affluent band of transatlantic English men and women, intent on high earning and high living, and I made a number of great English friends. One, in particular, became a very close friend with whom I used to 'party like it was 1999'. Her name was Sheila and, like me, she had just arrived in New York (in her case, from Los Angeles) as a manager for Armani. Sheila was like an older sister and we became solid partners in crime on the party circuit.

I was often visited by my brother Jerome on a break from his architectural studies in Rome and of course my father (frequently accompanied by my mother) would still visit regularly on business, so I did not feel that I was alone. For me, this was a golden time. I had a string of short romances but nothing serious. I enjoyed my bachelor-girl status and, having made so many friends, did not want to give up my independence. Sometimes, with my Walkman and my book, I would take the Staten Island ferry and lose myself in the music and the story, drinking in the feeling of just being in the place where I was born. I was never quite sure who to be – the gypsy girl from the Village with the deep intensity and the New Age books, or the legal eagle Uptown Girl that Billy Joel was singing about. Looking back, I believe that a university experience and the opportunity to travel are so important for young people. You have to walk a little on the wild side in order to find the balance.

Sheila and I, and our posse of pseudo-fashionista chicks,

would take revenge on the male of our species by lounging on the corner and watching all the boys go by. At that time Wall Street was awash with money, and man-watching over the top of our margaritas was a favourite way to pass an hour or two. We would eye up the investment bankers and the aspiring vice- and double-vice presidents, obsessing about the cut of their 'made-to-measure' suits, with custom colour linings, and their custom shirts, custom shoes and sports jackets with real buttonholes. Of course, all of these are things that most European thoroughbred males would have taken for granted. The Pan-European man will buy his suits in London (Savile Row, of course), his shirts in Paris and his shoes in Rome or Milan. Men at this time were particularly vain about their appearance – a positively 'beyond-the-era-of-the-dandy' image that my gay friends were so incisively cruel about. There is a code of esoteric detail to executive fashion that broadcasts hidden messages. The one that we girls saw most often in New York was 'See me, and know that I have made it'!

I did return to Italy for holidays, but my residency in America was long-term and I liked to travel around, exploring the 'Big Country'. On one occasion I will never forget, Sheila and I decided to get away from the party circuit and Studio 54, the famous Manhattan disco that we frequented. I had never been to Santa Fe in New Mexico, and Sheila knew of a fabulous health and beauty farm and spa there that she used to visit for time out when she lived in LA.

We shared a suite there, as bachelor girls do, to defray the cost of pampering, but I noticed that Sheila had become very tense. On the second day we went to visit the hot springs and took a bath together. All of a sudden Sheila began to cry. She just broke down and confessed that she had fallen in love with me. I was so shocked – I had not had the slightest idea. I was amazed that I could have been so blind and insensitive to her true feelings. The tragedy of the story is that I lost my best friend of that time. Her feelings for me made no difference to my regard for her but, after this confession, it became impossible for her to handle any sort of friendship. I never saw her again and that makes me sad, even to this day.

This crisis made me look deeply at myself and examine the spectrum of sexuality that is part of our unique identity. We know that with chemical therapy and surgery we can change sex; however, for me, the polarities found in a balanced sexuality (either heterosexual or homosexual) are nature's norm. Extremes of sexuality, in any relationship, are often a chemical recipe for tragedy – though they can also be the making of a creative genius. I can relate to this in terms of energies. I often have days and moods when I feel more feminine, and others when the male is raging within me. I believe that polarities are the basic forces of the universe; we ignore them at our peril.

By 1986 the US economy began shifting from rapid-growth recovery to a slower downturn. As 1987 came of age it seemed that recessionary fears might be premature, and that the boom times and boom city would continue. The property explosion of 1984 continued at a manic pace through 1986 but, by 1987, cracks had begun to appear. Business was brisk in our legal practice, but clients were edgy over volatile days on the markets. Monday has never been my favourite day, but Monday, 19 October 1987 is a day that will be imprinted on my brain for all time. This was the day the Dow Jones sank like a stone, by more than 22 per cent – the largest one-day fall ever seen in the US. A great deal of mystery surrounded the cause. There was no earth-shattering news or unprecedented event prior to the crash: the decline seemed to have come from nowhere. Some blamed the G7 rivalries, others overvaluation or the market psychology. Whatever the cause, I just have this overriding memory of the bizarre spectacle of the puppet Kermit the Frog giving an explanation of the day's events to the American people on national TV!

As I finished my Masters and began to further my career in the practice, I found myself asked to travel more often between Rome and New York on behalf of our international clients and their contracts. At the same time, the atmosphere in New York was changing. The crash of 1987 was followed by the bursting of the real-estate bubble in 1989, and the problems of foreign policy and the deteriorating situation in the Middle East were beginning to weigh down the spirit of America. There were still the distractions of the New York City Opera, the ballet, the public theatre and Broadway, my favourite drag for idle perambulation. Break-dancing, hip-hop culture and East Coast rap, however, were sleazing up and being tamed by media hype. Even the annual People's Poetry Gathering and the city poetry groups that I had loved to hang out at as a student had begun to pall. Could it be that I was falling out of love with New York, or was it just time for another change?

One of our key clients was the publisher of the only Italian newspaper in the US, *Il Progresso*. I was seconded to work on this account and, having always had an interest in journalism, found myself caught up in the coverage of the election campaign of George Herbert Walker Bush, Senior. This gave me the opportunity to understand how the paper was run. *Il Progresso* was funded by Italian-Americans and by the Italian government. In order to stay on top of things, I had to know what was going on politically in both Italy and the US. I became fascinated by public affairs and was introduced to the weird and wonderful world of the lobbyist.

I was still working on the real-estate side of the business so, between public affairs, property and travelling, I had little time to myself. I was dating at either end of the Rome to New York shuttle, but the so-called jet-set lifestyle had lost its glamour with the gruelling logistics involved in trying to run a life in two places at the same time. I decided that the 1980s 'material girl' was way past her sell-by date.

In 1989, world events began to escalate and the next couple of years saw the US invasion of Panama, the fall of the Soviet Union, followed by the invasion of oil-rich Kuwait by Saddam Hussein in his bid for dominance in the Middle East. I recall the newsflash when President Bush Senior addressed the Joint Session of Congress on 11 September 1990 and said to the world, 'Out of these troubled times, our fifth objective – a New World Order – can emerge: a new era.' These were the words that unleashed Operation Desert Storm, as the Gulf War of 1991 was known, and, even though I was a supporter of that war, I began to find my lay-over periods in Rome more exciting and the cultural climate more sympathetic to my mood. Political events in Italy were challenging and my intuition was calling me to a new decade of destiny.

As an American citizen, I can vote in the elections there, but I have to admit to being a real swing voter. I am part Republican and part Democrat. At heart, I guess, I am a liberal. My voting against George Bush Senior in the 1992 Presidential Election was due to the fact that I was a great admirer of Governor Bill Clinton of Arkansas. The Bush years were dogged by the tail-end of the 1980s recession – a major contributing factor to George Senior's defeat. I felt that change was needed to bring back some of the feel-good factor. Bill Clinton had the easy charm and charisma of a natural leader and he was an inspirational speaker. (As an aside, I have to say that I am also a great admirer of the Republican politician Rudy Giuliani – the ex-Mayor of New York – but when it comes to a new change of president in this post-millennium age, I would love to see a woman in office, or an African-American.)

Back then, in the summer of 1990, I decided to return to Rome for the time being. I was still undecided whether to move back permanently, or to take a brief sabbatical. Inevitably, I compromised and went back to work with my old legal firm in Rome, working in property law and public affairs, so that I would have six months to readjust to the old country with the option to travel to the US if and when the business dictated. Destiny was waiting in the wings.

ROMAN ROMANCE

●

A man whose eyes love opens risks his soul
His dancing breaks beyond the mind's control

THE CONFERENCE OF BIRDS (TRANSLATED FROM THE PERSIAN)

UI COMING BACK TO ROME, I FELT A NEW WAVE OF energy entering my life. This was a confusing time: I felt astride two worlds and quite uncertain of my path. I was tired of working in New York and felt I could rekindle the old magic if I took a break. I knew that I would have to listen out for my inner signal. I returned to my old law firm, the Studio Lupoi, to talk to my former professor about my future. I had been dealing with commercial law and the property sector for a number of years, but on advice from my professor, I thought it was time to choose an area that would give me more personal fulfilment as well as a rewarding career path. My experience of lobbying in the US had given me an interest in politics and public affairs, and the political climate in Italy in 1990 was in ferment. I began to feel that this might offer new and better prospects for my skills, so I decided to try to maintain my practice work but also to look for new options in the political world.

I enjoyed being back in Italy and being closer to my family. My father had been more or less retired for some years and he and my mother were living permanently in Apulia. My social life was low key and I spent time with my girlfriends and within the immediate circle of my work. One evening, just before the summer break, I went with my friend Irene to a party at one of her girlfriend's homes. I was relaxed, and felt I could let my hair down a little. I am used to making an entrance and when I arrived I was greeted with the usual Italian male charm offensive. The exception was a rather reserved man who remained looking bored and aloof in one corner of the room. Irene told me that this was the celebrated *notaio* Giancarlo Mazza, from one of Rome's biggest law firms.

This was how I met my first husband. There was no love at first sight. I was not struck by lightning – only by curiosity and the sense of being disarmed by this sensitive, mild-mannered man as I gravitated towards him. There was no pretence, no small-talk, and I was in no doubt that behind the mild manner lay a steely determination that only his eyes revealed. This was an experienced man, a safe harbour in whom I could trust and confide, and who knew the Italian legal system inside out. He came from a family long-established in the law and I was drawn to his quiet wisdom. I felt quite at ease with his clever conversation and we laughed often, almost as if we had known each other for many years.

You could see that this was a man who had suffered but did not resent his suffering. Later, I would learn that he was a single father and had had to bring up his three children on his own. I was fresh from New York, full of ideas, inquisitive about everything that was going on in Italy and eager to learn from a man of his experience. He was bored with the social round and seemed to be intrigued by this intense young woman with no agenda other than to extract as much information from him as possible and to have fun. There was absolutely no sexual chemistry at this stage, but we got on so well that we agreed to meet again after the summer break. As I left the party I had the feeling that I had found a new friend.

Giancarlo called me in September and we agreed to meet at his law firm to revisit the discussion on international operations that we had had when we first met. He was known to be broad-minded and open to new ideas. I had pursued a very varied period of study and work experience, and one of my secret ambitions was to start my own practice and specialize in women's legal issues. I had visions of working on high-profile cases with lady partners.

I will not forget how Giancarlo said he found women the nobler sex and that, in terms of a perception of human power-play, women had the greater discrimination. He said, 'Given the choice between conversation with a man or a woman of the same education, I would always choose the woman. It is hard to be bored in the company of women. Even gossip is educational.' I think from then on I realized that I was dealing with a very unusual man – a man who, I later understood, had studied the psychology of human interaction and was an avid reader of the classical esoteric (as opposed to the New Age) books. We went out for dinner several times and continued the slow burn of our friendship. Nothing more physical was on the menu. But a marriage of true minds is like an alchemical fire: it can ignite the elements of passion.

This was a fascinating time to be observing public affairs in Italy in the undefined role of a lobbyist. During the 1980s, whilst I was away in America, Silvio Berlusconi had built his media group, Mediaset, into a countrywide network of local TV stations with uniform programming that had very effectively created a single national station. The only problem was that this was illegal, as the monopoly on national TV broadcasting was reserved for the public service broadcaster, RAI. The courts moved to block Berlusconi and dismantle his broadcasting empire. But Berlusconi was a very smart operator and had forged strong links with Bettino Craxi, secretary-general of the Italian Socialist Party and Prime Minister of Italy at that time. Controversially, Craxi legalized the national TV broadcasts made by Berlusconi's channels.

In the early 1990s, Berlusconi turned his attention to politics and set about establishing a new party. In 1986 he had purchased the famous AC Milan football club as part of his empire, and he now used the independent fan clubs of the team as a model for building up a network of political supporters. A master of public relations, he even adopted the AC Milan supporters' chant, Forza Italia – Go Italy – as the party's name, thus turning the existing network of football fans to his political advantage. Just as AC Milan fan clubs had sprung up around the country, so groups of Forza Italia supporters were founded or spontaneously appeared in many places.

The two largest political parties – the Christian Democrats (Democrazia Cristiana) and the Socialist Party (Partito Socialista Italiano) – had been tarnished by criminal investigations into financial corruption by leading party members. In January 1994, with the elections approaching, Silvio Berlusconi announced his decision to 'enter the field' and stand for election on a platform aimed at the defeat of communism. His campaign was born in controversy, as investigators into the *Mani pulite* ('clean hands') affair, involving corruption linked to the financing of political parties and the alleged bribing of judges, were about to issue warrants for his arrest. This was my initiation into the turbulent world of the new Italian politics, and the background to my falling in love with my husband-to-be.

The more I learned about Giancarlo, the more I respected him. He had been through so much with the break-up of his marriage and the responsibility of raising his family alone. He had never thought about getting married again and had immersed himself in psychological studies and the practice of a new form of meditation. When I arrived from New York, his children were more or less grown up. At the time of his divorce his younger boy had been just three; when Giancarlo and I met, he was eighteen. The boys were keen to fly the nest and his daughter Chiara was about to get married.

After a while our friendship blossomed into a relationship based on trust and a shared sense of life and values. Our age difference made no difference to me: I had always been attracted to older men. Perhaps unconsciously I was looking for a father figure, but I never thought of my relationship with Giancarlo in this way. He was the right person at the right time for that stage of my life. In just being with him I found a sense of security unlike any other I had known. As 1991 wore on we began to date and, for the first time, I felt that I might be falling in love.

We both loved the Roman habit of the baths and decided to visit the famous Thermae Saturnia in Tuscany – just a couple of hours' drive from Rome – for a 1991 New Year's Eve break. I think this was the tipping point in our romance and we both knew that a new phase in our lives had begun. I little dreamed then that within only a few years the Thermae Saturnia would open yet another chapter in my life – a chapter that would lead me to the love of my life and to England.

At the top of his profession, tired of being a single parent and with his children leaving home, Giancarlo wanted a new climate in his life. I, too, had realized that what I was missing was the security of a long-term loving relationship. Giancarlo called me his 'holiday', meaning that the time we spent together was freedom from the cares of the world. And so we found together a relationship that gave us both a 'holiday' from the world and, true to the holiday idea, we took time to travel a lot. We began to live together in 1992 when we bought a house, wanting everything to be new, and I took on the renovation project. Giancarlo was already established so, within reason, he could do what he liked. We travelled around the world twice, in different directions, and made an intellectual feast of art exhibitions, concerts and theatres. The balance of career and relationship was weighted heavily in favour of quality time together. Then, my world was turned upside down. I fell pregnant.

Nature's time is often not the time we would choose, and in this case the timing was all wrong. We were not married and I still felt I was too young. I had ambitions for my career and our relationship was too new. We needed more time to settle into life together and a child at this time would not have been right for the child, for Giancarlo or for me. I was torn between biology and my sense of self. Instinctively, I wanted the child – but I wasn't ready. Was it fair to bring a child into the world under the shadow of possible resentment? Also, most importantly for me, I did not want Giancarlo thinking I was forcing his hand into an immediate marriage. I was scared, and the endless turning over of options in my mind and imagination made me depressed. In hindsight, making the decision to terminate was liberating in a way, although so difficult at the time. I took the decision on the basis of what I believed to be good for the relationship, not for any emotional advantage. Although I am comfortable with that decision to this day, later, when we separated, Giancarlo regretted not having stopped me. But children are no guarantee of love and I have no regrets. Nevertheless, the physical trauma of such a loss always affects a woman's emotional constitution. In my case I chose to suppress my biology and focus on my career and my new relationship to take my mind off the pain.

Around this time a team of Milan judges began investigating the affairs of party financing and the government of Italy went into meltdown. Key figures in both government and industry were forced to resign in disgrace over alleged corruption, kickbacks and vote rigging. Giancarlo and I watched it all with interest and discussed the opportunities for me to set up my own lobbying and public affairs office, based on my work between the US and Italy. The conflicts of interest between Italian politics and business were so blatant that it called for urgent reform. I wanted to make that difference.

Silvio Berlusconi is a larger-than-life character who has always attracted controversy. When he founded Forza Italia in 1993, just when he was about to be arrested, there were nationwide debates about his motivation. His detractors accused him of abusing the system by claiming immunity from prosecution. His supporters, meanwhile, branded him as the 'new man' from outside the system who could reform the corrupt and inefficient public bureaucracy. The aim of Forza

Italia was to attract all those moderate voters who were feeling disillusioned and unrepresented. Berlusconi also promised to bring more women into government – something I was passionate about – and I was impressed by his obvious genius for communications. At the time I was working with the Italian parliament as a lobbyist for the chairman of the Financial Commission, which I found fascinating. The executive director of the old legal practice that I had worked for in Milan, Vittorio Dotti, had for a long time been Berlusconi's lawyer and now was also a rising star in Forza Italia. It was only natural that he would take me under his wing. I never dreamed that he might be grooming me for office and that just two years later he would ask me to stand as a candidate for election to the Assembly of Rome.

I think Giancarlo realized before I did that my active role in politics might lead to a call for me to work on the launch of any future national campaign. We had lived together now for over a year and found our relationship had grown in closeness and intensity. This was a time of deep personal satisfaction. I had a great career working to make a difference in the world and I was in love. Then I fell pregnant for a second time.

No decision had been made to start a family and we had not been trying for a child. Once again, it just happened. Although Giancarlo had said he wanted children, I was not sure that I did at that time. We were both a little bit in shock but, as the full realization dawned, Giancarlo was over the moon. Although not convinced, I began to resign myself to the inevitable. I had thought that, as he already had three children of his own and had had to bring them up as a single father, he would be tired of the burden of child-raising and that as his 'holiday' he might want me all to himself. As it was, he was happy for both of us. I began to experience the biological ups and downs of an expectant mother. My career in politics looked to be short. Then, after just two months, I had a miscarriage.

The psychological trauma of the miscarriage was very different to that of the termination, when the conscious decision had made it easier to bear the pain. Now I felt sad and physically very low. Giancarlo was a very sensitive man and naturally very upset, both for me and for the loss of the child. Later, when I left him, I think he thought that had we had children I might have stayed. I am not sure if I believe that. Although a duty is a binding commitment, often love and passion will drive a coach and horses through our best intentions. For some women the biological bond to their children is stronger than their love for their man; for others the man will always come first. Had I had children, perhaps my responsibilities might have determined my future actions. We will never know. The decision to have a baby had not been made consciously, but I had been happy with the accident of life. Now I was sad to lose a second chance at having a child, but I felt that again life had made the decision for me. I hadn't been ready for such a big change and was content with a family of just the two of us. I was still young and there was plenty of time to expand my family. One day we would try again.

When the call to help with the development of the programme for Forza Italia's election campaign came, I knew this would be an opportunity for me to rise again from the ashes of my unhappy experience. Events moved fast once the party had been founded and my job would be to help develop and run the national campaign. I think Giancarlo knew we would be in for a roller-coaster ride once the campaign was launched. As a deeply spiritual man who had had a very formal religious upbringing, I think he felt that it was time to formalize our commitment to each other in a conventional way. Maybe the shared pain of our loss made him want to make things better for me. We had lived together for two years, but when he asked me to marry him, in his most sweet and formal manner, my heart responded before I could speak and tears came to my eyes. The only answer I could give was the full kiss of assent.

The astonishing fact about the meteoric rise of Silvio Berlusconi was that Forza Italia was set up only a few months before his election victory in March 1994. His strategy of using the football fan base as a model for securing political support was underpinned by a massive publicity campaign broadcast via his television and communications network. After all the scandals and corruption that had soured and discredited Italian politics, he seemed to provide a clear and inclusive path to making the country as prosperous and successful as he had made himself. Berlusconi referred to himself as a 'man of *all* the people', from industrial workers to farmers to businessmen and intellectuals. The massive public participation seemed to offer a fresh start, and even old and seasoned campaigners like my husband felt he might indeed provide a new way. My work as a coordinator of the national campaign in Rome gave me a front-row position in the game and one could only admire his '*Berlusconismo*' as a winning formula.

So began a love affair with the world of politics that would put the metal of my womanhood to the test when I was later persuaded to stand as a candidate myself. The grounding in politics that I gained on the campaign and the first-hand experience of working with the PR genius Silvio Berlusconi made me realize the immense social power of football as a force to influence people – especially young people.

I really understood how different Berlusconi was at the first party convention I attended. He often had his stage make-up touched up, to keep up a good impression, just like an actor. One thing he said particularly sticks in my mind. In a talk about how we should present ourselves as party representatives, he told us, 'Everyone you meet must be happy to have met you.' He obviously applied this to everything he did and it was extremely effective.

In February 1994, just as we were launching the national campaign, Silvio Berlusconi received formal notice that he would be under legal investigation for alleged involvement in political and financial corruption. Later, when he was Prime

Minister, he called for a block on this type of legal action, charging the judiciary with trying to 'overthrow the results of the popular vote'. This is a difficult dilemma: while I do not believe that judges should be able to undermine the electorate, I have never been in favour of politicians being immune from prosecution and therefore above the law: it is a licence for lack of accountability and corruption.

Berlusconi's combative relationship with the judiciary has been endless, but I had to admire the sheer energy and charisma of a man with the self-confidence to talk his way out of trouble believing that only he could turn Italy around. The elections were a landslide, with Forza Italia taking the lion's share of the popular vote – 21 per cent, the highest percentage of any single party. In the campaign office we all felt very proud of ourselves.

When my campaign work was over, Giancarlo urged me to take some time out to start making practical arrangements for our wedding. He wanted to marry me in church, as I was the love of his life, or at least he believed so at the time. It is a sad fact for us Catholics that once you are divorced that privilege is no longer possible without special consent from the Church. There is a loophole if you can have your marriage annulled, which in Italy means you have to go before a special tribunal of the Church called '*La Sacra Rota*'. The grounds are narrow and well defined: there are about as many ways to get a marriage annulled as there are to enter the Kingdom of Heaven. Giancarlo hated the idea of not being married in a church, but personally I never thought it was that important. I have always loved a church atmosphere with incense and choirs, but under the circumstances I was just as happy to marry in a beautiful civil setting and have a wonderful party.

If we were going to have a civil wedding, Giancarlo and I were determined to make it as sacred an experience as possible. We organized a private blessing for our marriage with the Bishop of Rome, who was a friend of Giancarlo's. But, for the ceremony itself, the best place I could think of was to return to the heart of the city in which I was born. Rather like the choice of Windsor Registry Office by Prince Charles and Camilla Parker Bowles as a place of special significance for their marriage, so New York City Hall was ours. The time I love best in New York is Christmas and New Year. To keep faith with both the European and the American themes of our life, we decided to spend Christmas in Switzerland and to marry in Manhattan in the New Year. Come December, however, fate dealt from the bottom of the deck for our wedding plans.

Always in the background were continuing political upheavals. Berlusconi had secured his election victory by forging alliances between Forza Italia and the Lega Nord (Northern League) and Alleanza Nazionale (National Alliance), who were not linked to each other. It was an uneasy coalition and proved to be shortlived. After only seven months, the government fell in December.

The first part of our wedding plans went well and our

Christmas in Switzerland was as magical as only snow and sleighbells can be. Unfortunately, when we arrived at the Mayfair Hotel in New York ahead of our guests, hoping to see in a fabulous New Year, Giancarlo was taken seriously ill with an internal haemorrhage. As a result, he had to spend New Year's Eve in hospital. I was very worried, but Giancarlo is a tough man and he would not let the illness defeat him. Despite family protest, he was up within days and ready to carry on. In spite of all the drama, our wedding took place as planned on 3 January 1995. We couldn't wait for our honeymoon in Anguilla and the chance to relax away from the world. We had a wonderful reception dinner at Le Cirque – the well-known Manhattan restaurant – knowing that we would be hosting a further reception in Rome when we returned. I had wanted just a quiet family affair in New York, and the atmosphere was very intimate and understated. This was just what was needed, as Giancarlo was still weak from his surgery. Although my parents had been very wary of my relationship with Giancarlo at first, they were pleased to see me so happy. As they got to know him better, they grew to love him and welcome him into the family.

I wanted our Roman reception to be a once-in-a-lifetime experience. We decided to have something completely different to celebrate our union with our family and friends in Italy. We chose as the backdrop for our day a fabulous sixteenth-century palazzo close to the Piazza Navona. I have always loved the movies, so I chose our favourite offbeat film from the era of the greats as the theme for the day. The film was *Il Gattopardo – The Leopard –* starring Burt Lancaster, Alain Delon and the fabulous Claudia Cardinale at her height.

My dress was styled on Claudia Cardinale's costume from the film and was designed by the fabulous Gattinoni, who was then eighty-nine, and who, during her career, had dressed Princess Margaret and Grace Kelly. My dress was to be her last. We had requested the live orchestra from the Auditorium in Rome and the guests arrived to be greeted by flowers and music. Later my friends told me that when our arrival was announced to the assembled guests a hush fell on the reception room. Then the first violin struck up. I will never forget the melody of that violin as Giancarlo and I made our entrance – dancing. For me this was a magical moment: I felt that I was dancing the dance of life. It was one of the happiest days of my life. I will always be grateful to Giancarlo for this gift and for the wonderful years we shared within a marriage of true minds.

The spring of 1995 was a period of local administrative elections. We had just returned from our European honeymoon when the call came from my old friend and mentor, Vittorio Dotti. One of the founding policies of Forza Italia that had attracted me to the party was its proposals for greater opportunities for women in politics. I had always been cynical about women's access to and influence in the male-dominated party system. A good indicator of party gender reform is the number of women within leadership structures and their inclusion in decision-making. The final test is commitment to the participation of women in leadership and elected political positions. In Italy this was low. When I was asked to stand as a candidate for the Regional Assembly of Rome, the offer was too attractive to turn down. Naive idealism and political ambitions won over the temptation to be a lady of leisure, enjoying life at home as a newly-wed with my husband. I resolved to stand as a candidate for Rome.

Looking back at my candidacy persona from the perspective of the second half of the first decade of the new millennium, I feel rather proud of her. She may have been naive and idealistic, but I think that trends in world politics today have proved that her intuition was right. Electorates around the world demonstrate a large lack of faith and respect in political parties. We constantly see flawed electoral systems encourage corruption and the abuse of power. Many radical activists focus their attention on transnational corporations as the villains of the modern world. From my perspective, the real failure in the modern world is the failure of government and the abuse of the United Nations as a forum for state interests rather than for global governance and the rule of international law. My initiation came early.

Having done much of my legal training in America, I always had a deep respect for the direct primary election system. This means that candidates for elective office in the US are selected by voters rather than by party leaders. I was greatly in favour of democratizing candidate selection in Italy. Many countries in Europe operate their selection procedures on a cartel basis, although this is changing today. In the UK both the Labour and Conservative parties have recently reformed their selection procedures, and now operate what Americans would call a restricted primary system in which candidates are selected by a vote limited to party members. In Italy, at the time of my selection to stand, the system was run like a cartel and candidates had their respective political Godfathers. I was no exception.

As an idealistic young woman excited by the thrill of political manoeuvring, I thought I could change the system and decided to campaign on a programme for greater democracy within the selection process. Little did I realize that this would be a quick way to lose friends and win enemies. Furthermore, I was a woman. Despite the controversy, I was popular, being seen as one of the new forces for change. At that time I believed in change from within – but you don't take on the establishment without paying a price. In the weeks to come I would pay that price and, later, so would my protector, Vittorio Dotti.

I knew Cesare Previti from my time working for the launch of the national campaign in 1994. The Milan court later ruled that Deputy Previti had 'corrupted' the judges in Rome in 1991 in order to facilitate Berlusconi's acquisition of Italy's largest publishing house, Mondadori. Previti was under the patronage of Berlusconi, who wanted him to serve as Minister of Justice in his first cabinet, but the President of the Republic, Oscar Luigi Scalfaro, opposed the appointment due to Previti's alleged shady dealings. As a compromise with Berlusconi, who had defended his record, Previti was appointed Minister of Defence. His term had come to an end by the time the local elections were due to be held and he became the political sponsor of those who opposed me. My enduring memory of Cesare Previti is his arrival behind the scenes at Casina Valadier (once the home of Paolina Borghese, Napoleon Bonaparte's sister), the operations centre for the launch of the national campaign. Perhaps he could sense my antipathy, or maybe I was not overdeferential, but his manner had irritated me as much as mine had irritated him. I could not respect his conduct and from then on I felt he made it his business to undermine my election campaign and secure victory for his chosen favourites. This experience only served to confirm my belief in open primaries without party obligation.

My brief twenty-day campaign seemed to last a lifetime. During the build-up I saw it all, and working overtime even put my relationship on the line. I know it may seem melodramatic from the point of view of those who have come to know my public persona from a later incarnation, but at the time the fight felt like a struggle between the forces of darkness and light. I lost count of the number of people coming to my door to offer their vote. The requests for money or for favours were not even thinly veiled. The voting system had also changed since 1994, reverting back to the old pro-portional system, and voters had to write their names against their selected candidate – always an intimidating prospect. My posters were all over Rome and the new kid on the block received a lot of genuine public support. I fought a valiant campaign and an unofficial exit poll gave me the result. But in the end it was not to be. The forces of the party establishment and the fixed interests triumphed. I decided that for the moment my political game was over.

My one enduring achievement from my time in politics, of which I am very proud, is that I opened the debate on procedural fairness for candidate selection and the need for greater democracy. In the lead-up to my campaign, I had invited a distinguished friend and professor from my student days in America, Edward Luttwak, to be guest speaker at a conference to introduce Italian party members to the primary selection process in the US. The issue never went away, even after I left politics. The principle was adopted by the centre-left and Romano Prodi championed the reform of the internal selection process. Now, the centre-right is also moving in that direction, as is the whole of the European Union. I am glad that my political adventure planted a seed for the future.

My return to our house on the Via dei Monti Parioli in the aftermath of the election furore made me realize the value of home. Our house was a sanctuary and just being back with my husband without being beholden to anyone made me feel like a human being again. In life you are never quite satisfied until you have been down the 'there and back again' road. Being somebody is just as tiresome as being nobody. When you have it you take it for granted; when you don't you will die for it. When you finally get whatever it was you wanted in the first place, it is never quite as good as the expectation. But it is only when you experience things that you know you are alive.

What then of Silvio Berlusconi? You have to admire the first serving Prime Minister of Italy to appear at his own trial and say, 'I stand before court with an untarnished reputation.' His claim is true. Despite all the investigations and trials, Berlusconi has never been convicted on any charges of bribery or corruption. His charm and charisma are legendary – as are his cheesy chat-up lines and bad jokes – and he is a genius at making people forgive him his faults. I was disappointed by his later attitude to women: he started out with so much promise in this area when I first worked with Forza, but in the end the centre-left gave more opportunities to women than his centre-right. Recently his wife, Veronica Lario, took a front page in *La Repubblica* to complain about some louche quips her now seventy-year-old husband made at a recent television awards ceremony. His response was immediate: a charming declaration of love streamed across the Italian media – yet another example of why Berlusconi remains one of the most extravagant personalities in Italian politics today.

THE YEAR OF LOVING DANGEROUSLY

•

Let me not to the marriage of true minds
Admit impediments. Love is not love
Which alters when it alteration finds,
Or bends with the remover to remove;
O no! it is an ever-fixed mark,
That looks on tempests and is never shaken;
It is the star to every wandering bark,
Whose worth's unknown, although his height be taken.
Love's not Time's fool, though rosy lips and cheeks
Within his bending sickle's compass come;
Love alters not with his brief hours and weeks,
But bears it out even to the edge of doom.
If this be error and upon me proved,
I never writ, nor no man ever loved.

WILLIAM SHAKESPEARE, SONNET CXVI

VII ONE OF THE MOST DIFFICULT ASPECTS OF PUBLIC life is the loss of the feeling of control when the bubble bursts. When the oxygen of attention is denied, the experience can be a major source of distress for celebrities. This is true from whichever stable you come – political party, TV network, football club or plain old leader of the pack. The habit of notoriety can make us all a little precious and self-important. I always admire those in the public eye who can remain true to themselves at all times and are not affected by the heady intoxication of being the centre of attention. I have usually found that those who display this strength of character have been well loved from birth and have friends and family who will not put up with airs and graces. I count myself lucky in that way and when my political adventure came to an end I felt a huge sense of relief that my life could go back to normal.

My husband knew that I loved the sea and had always liked boats since my youth in the fishing villages of Apulia. He may have felt I needed a little cheering up after the lacerating experience of party politics. The soothing balm was not just liberally applied holidays, complete with massage oil, but came as an anniversary gift in the form of a fabulous 27-metre-long, custom-built motor cruiser we called the *Nancy One*. She was a classic, wooden-built angel of a boat and had been the darling of a Neapolitan businessman. So my husband and I began our halcyon time. We loved to cruise the Mediterranean, free to go where we wished – the Côte d'Azur, Sardinia and, my favourite cruise of all, the Greek islands. I love to cruise by candlelight under the full moon, with the sound of the water and the clink of rigging. For me this is real freedom and the wonderful feeling of summer.

There was also sadness mingled with our joy and excitement at having the *Nancy One*. After we bought her, we spent months refitting and refurbishing her and decided to throw a family party to inaugurate her. Amongst the guests, my brother Jerome and his new girlfriend were invited from New York as we were keen to meet her. At the time, Jerry was doing some work as an architect on a project for the Valentino fashion house in Paris. The plan was for them both to join us on the boat – Jerome had flown in already and his girlfriend was to fly to Paris from the US then on to meet up with us. Tragically, she never made it as the plane she was on crashed.

Of course, all the family were devastated and I don't think Jerry ever really recovered.

When we returned to Rome after the summer holidays I knew I had to pick up the pieces of my legal consultancy work. After the political turmoil I had experienced, the ups and downs of property law and real-estate contract work were a much less onerous routine. I did some work with the Bourse – the stock exchange – and carried on advising Italian corporations with commercial contracts in the United States. Gradually, my husband and I began to realize that our private life was more important than my career. At different stages in your life you have different priorities and we decided we needed more quality time together to do the things we wanted to do for ourselves. We worked together on our property portfolio and I found the balance of involvement in our private projects and being a home-maker worked well for me. I loved to visit the antique shops and art galleries of Rome and had more leisure time to collect individual works and to pursue my cultural interests. Our house became a rather exotic think-tank and my dinner parties, with an eclectic mix of film directors, artists, poets and politicians, were famous as incubators for ideas. I was younger than many society ladies, and my gay friends would tease me about my terrace dinners and call me the 'Princess of Rome'. I was comfortable with my life and happier than I could remember.

So our life passed comfortably from 1996 into 1997 and my career was all but on hold. Giancarlo and I travelled nearly every weekend and I had all the things that a woman in her early thirties could desire. Perhaps I became too indolent, or tired of all the good times having good times; whatever the reason, my skin began to itch with the need to change things and move on. I will never know if there was an unconscious undercurrent or a need for something new. I was not bored, yet neither was I challenged.

I have had the privilege of living so many lives in one life. I often feel that both people and events are like doors into a parallel universe. Maybe that is what attracts us to the thrill of the new. Even now, when I reflect back, I have no explanation for the path along which destiny would lead me in the coming months. I was content in my marriage and had no flirtations or extramarital interest of any kind. The idea of an affair was something I discussed with my husband as a thing that happened in other people's lives. If an affair happens, it means either something has gone wrong or is missing in a relationship, or, as in my case, you meet an irresistible attraction – that is, you fall in love.

As you can see from my story so far, football didn't really figure in my life. My husband was a Roma fan and Lazio was my stepson's favourite team. As an Italian, I knew about football but looked upon it as a sport of the arena. I used to watch the national games and my club side was Juventus – but my interest was fickle. My single biggest involvement had been observing Silvio Berlusconi develop his master strategy for founding his political power on the football-club model

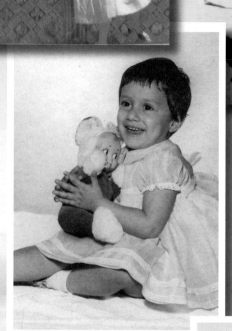

Top left: *My mother on holiday in Italy in the 1950s before she met my father.*

Above: *My father at his uncle's ranch in Frezno, California soon after arriving in America.*

Left: *Me in my parents' apartment in New York, aged two.*

Right: *With my father in Apulia.*

Left: *My first holiday to Italy, aged two. We were on a trip to Capri with my cousins. I am sitting on the bench with my mother.*

Left: *At kindergarten in New York, aged four.*

Right: *My mother, brother Jerome and me during our voyage from New York to Italy.*

Below: *At my parents' villa in Bisceglie, aged ten.*

Above: *With my father and Jerome at Italy in Miniature, a theme park near Rimini.*

Left: *On the balcony of our apartment while on holiday in Positano with my parentss.*

Above: *Performing in my ballet school's annual competition.*

Right: *On a family skiing trip to Cortina.*

In my first year of university.

Above: *The World Trade Center, which caught my imagination while I was studying in New York in the 1980s.*

Right: *At the Rockefeller Plaza whilst doing a term at university in New York for extra credits.*

Far right: *At a party in New York after graduating from my masters.*

Left: *With my brother Jerome when he accompanied me on a business trip to the Caribbean.*

Above: *On a trip to Jordan during my travels with Giancarlo.*

Right: *Ready to go to a masked ball with Giancarlo during the Venice Carnival.*

Below: *With my father at my parents' villa in Apulia where we were celebrating my grandmother's 100th birthday.*

Above: *A picture from my wedding party in Rome in the Gattopardo dress.*

Left: *Aboard the Nancy One.*

Right: *Our mosquito-infested trip to Sweden in 1998. The group included Giancarlo and Sven.*

A CINQUE ANNI DAL DUEMILA E'ORA DI PENSARE AL FUTURO DEL PAESE

My election pamphlet from my candidature for Forza Italia in Rome.

NANCY DELL'OLIO

ALLA REGIONE.

PERCHE' CREDIAMO ALLA FORZA DELLE IDEE.

PERCHE' SONO LE PERSONE CHE FANNO LA DIFFERENZA.

Nancy Dell'Olio ha 32 anni ed è nata a New York. Sposata con il notaio Giancarlo Mazza, risiede e lavora a Roma.
Laureata in Legge con una tesi in diritto privato comparato e il massimo dei voti, si specializza alla Columbia University e l'anno seguente consegue il Master in Diritto societario e finanziario alla New York University Law School.
Dal 1986 collabora con alcuni tra i più noti studi legali di Roma e New York, e con società operanti in Italia, in Europa e negli Stati Uniti.
Parla correntemente inglese, francese e spagnolo.
Negli ultimi anni ha collaborato con l'Ufficio legislativo del Senato e della Camera dei Deputati, sia per la Legge finanziaria, sia per la preparazione di disegni di legge riguardanti lo sviluppo delle piccole e medie imprese, il lavoro, l'ambiente e i portatori di handicap.
Convinta che tutti devono fare la propria parte per contribuire al rinnovamento delle Istituzioni e allo sviluppo del Paese, si è impegnata fin dall'inizio nella organizzazione di Forza Italia, partecipando attivamente alla vita politica del Movimento a Roma e nella sua provincia.
E' stata tra le promotrici di un recente convegno sui sistemi elettorali in Italia e negli Usa.
Tra i suoi obiettivi, l'introduzione delle primarie per la scelta diretta dei candidati da parte dei cittadini, per rendere la politica sempre più trasparente e vicina alle esigenze e ai problemi della gente.

of building a supporters' network. So, when my husband pointed out the new football manager for Lazio at a table in our favourite restaurant in Thermae Saturnia, I could not have been less interested. In fact, I hadn't noticed him at all. My husband and our friends had known all about Lazio's new Swedish coach from his earlier days at Roma, and I watched as Giancarlo and a friend walked over to greet him. As they neared his table I had the distinct sense of being stared at. This was my first eye contact with Sven-Goran Eriksson. He looked vaguely academic and inscrutable behind his glasses.

I knew immediately he was looking at me and I felt a little curiosity at the level of intensity. Later he told me that he was completely transfixed from the first moment he saw me. He couldn't show it – and yet he could not keep his gaze from me. I was used to men's admiration, and audacious eye language is part of the Italian charm. This was very different. There was no doubt that he felt an immediate attraction. He looked quite distinguished but nothing special. I believe in a spiritual connection, but our encounter had given me no intuitive reading. My husband was delighted to have met him and found him very courteous and cultured.

The meeting at the Thermae was in October and Sven had been taking a weekend break away from Rome as the national team were playing. Having recently arrived at Lazio, he had been testing his team formations. Building a strong new team was his first priority. Sven had gained the confidence of club owner Sergio Cragnotti, and together they were putting together a great combination of talent. Cragnotti was a multi-millionaire businessman with great connections in the banking sector and had bought into massive food-processing companies like Cirio and Del Monte. He went on to purchase Lazio in 1992 and was a very ambitious and astute operator. He had a big chequebook and was generous in support of his managers.

Sven and I met again as he joined our circle for one or two dinner parties at our house, but then we received an invitation from him to his birthday celebration. A big party had been organized – 5 February 1998 – at Bella Blu, a Roman equivalent of the London club Annabel's, with live music. My husband and I walked in for dinner to find the party table in full swing. Things were going well at Lazio with an unbeaten run and Sven was looking forward to the arrival of Chile's Marcelo Salas, fresh from defeating England at Wembley.

Again I felt those ice-blue Nordic eyes lock on to me. I noticed a look of shock mixed with desire, which came across as shy overattentiveness verging on obsession. A woman can almost always tell when a man is looking at her with desire. Some are subtle, others are vulgar and there is a big difference between a gaze of admiration and one of violation. I knew Sven was attracted to me, but he did not cross the line and was always the gentleman. For the first time there was chemistry, although I could not admit that to myself then. With him was his daughter, Lina, and his ex-wife Ann-Christin – they had broken up in 1994 after seventeen years of marriage. Women are very intuitive and I think that she picked up on the attraction he felt, although there was nothing overt in his manner. My husband congratulated him on his progress with Lazio and there was a light-hearted mood all round. Still his eyes searched for mine; even with my back to him I could feel the white-hot laser of his stare. I think, for Sven, that that night was *the* night: that maybe this woman was 'the one'. For my part, I was not conscious of anything strong, except the magnetic curiosity of a woman who knows she has ignited the passion of an exceptional man. An alchemy in attraction.

At this time our communication was entirely subliminal. I loved my husband and had never contemplated any other relationship. Even if I had been aware of an attraction, I would have denied it. My husband had liked Sven from the start and, after our second meeting, felt it would only be natural to draw him into our social circle. Meetings by chance are the way fate spins our lives towards a path we do not consciously choose.

My husband was a kind man with a mind that was always open to new experiences and new people. Naturally, he wanted to include Sven in our lives as a new friend. My initial indifference had turned to a casual interest since our last encounter and Lazio continued to do well. Lazio became the first Italian club to be floated on the Bourse on 19 March 1998. The flotation was so successful that the volume of share trading caused the computer to crash. My husband and I held a dinner at our club and Sven was invited as part of our round table of interesting people. We were both delighted when he accepted.

Once again he saw me before I saw him; I became aware of his presence only after feeling what seemed like an invisible force willing me to notice him. We watched for each other across the crowded room and, as we circled towards each other, we both felt we were being drawn together. When, finally, we stood in front of each other, neither of us could think of what to say. After a few mumbled pleasantries I heard myself ask, 'Would you like to have lunch sometime?'

'What am I doing?' I thought in shock. 'I am a married woman.'

I think he was as surprised as I was at my invitation. I was behaving right out of character.

Later Sven joked that this was to be the longest lunch date he ever had to wait for. I took a month to decide. It was mid-April before I found the courage to meet him. When I called him he was totally surprised and said, 'I thought you were never going to call – I'm so glad you have.'

I was still very nervous and not quite sure what I was doing or why I was doing it. 'Where would you like to go for lunch?' I asked.

He answered without hesitation, in the way that only a man who values his privacy would do. He suggested his own house as we might find the attention too much in a public place. There are very few men who might have a plausible reason for such an invitation, but he was one of them and our situation would be a little unusual. I detected a hint of amusement in his voice, mixed with the excitement of anticipation. Football managers have impossible diaries, so once the day was chosen I knew that we would have to stick to it. I had a week to choose if I wished to cancel or not. What stress!

Waking up on the day of the date was bad enough. I had suppressed the whole question of whether this was the right thing to do. I changed my mind three times and almost rang to cancel. And, even in the taxi on the way over to Sven's house, I nearly turned back.

This was the beginning of our love story. The lunch was like a dream. We both realized the intensity of the passion was beyond our control. We were both scared, knowing that we were embarking on something that might be the cause of huge changes in our lives. The attraction was electric before we touched – one touch was all it took.

I was surprised at myself. You follow the flow of life instinctively and then you have to live with the consequences. For Sven it was already completely clear. He wanted us to be together as often as possible. For me the emotional confusion was troubling. I loved my husband and did not want to hurt him, and yet I was in the tempest of a new relationship – a passion that set my soul on fire and made my body electric. I like to think that our passion seemed to give new inspiration to Sven and to Lazio. Despite disappointment in the League, they reached the final of the Italian Cup, and after dismissing

Roma, Napoli and Juventus, they faced Milan. This was the beginning of my new interest in football. The cup final was the first of Sven's matches that I went to watch. I went with my girlfriend Marcella, who was a great fan of Lazio, and my husband was amused and not unduly concerned by my sudden interest in football. I had been surprised and delighted when the tickets arrived accompanied by a beautiful note from Sven. This became a habit of his, so I had to keep a sharp eye on the post. Sven was delighted that I had come to the game. Lazio had been in a long trophy drought, so winning the cup was a turn of fortune to be toasted with champagne. This was also the beginning of what would be the long hot summer of love for us.

When you are in love, time apart is like torture. Sven and I did not have much time to see each other. I was married and we were both well-known figures in Roman society. We could not really be free together in public. Everything just seemed to happen in the space of a few months. Our best time to meet was at lunch time and Sven gave up his tennis to be with me. He loves his tennis, so of course I appreciated that this was no small 'sacrifice', but this was his only time free from club duties. The universe seemed to lend us a cloak of invisibility: no one knew what was going on. We shared together a sweet complicity in the planning of our clandestine meetings, knowing that they would be few and far between. Because they were so few, the times we spent together are etched in my memory for ever.

Lazio's progress towards the UEFA Cup semi-final had not stretched them too far. A win against Atlético in Madrid took them through to an all-Italian final at which they would meet old rivals, Inter Milan, in Paris. I was like a moth to a flame. My stepson was an ardent Lazio supporter and when the excuse came, heaven sent, to go to Paris to watch the match, he and his son accompanied me. We were guests of the club, staying in the same hotel as Sven. I took them both to meet the team and was able to see Sven for a few minutes. In a strange way, although we were not together, just being in the same hotel at the same time with our secret love affair brought a feeling of peace to my feverish heart.

There was a fantastic atmosphere at the match. From the start Inter seemed the most sure of the two teams, but of course it was a bitter disappointment for all of us when they triumphed. When Sven came very late to join our group of friends after dinner, I could not help but admire his sangfroid. I felt very sad and saw for the first time how losing a game at this level can be so hard. Sven said that naturally he was disappointed, but getting to the final had been a great achievement. I will never forget his final words before going back to his room: 'When you win you win, but when you lose it's how you lose that is important.' As he walked away from our group I felt very proud of this quiet man I had come to love.

Our first real escape away together was to Positano, the beautiful resort on the Amalfi Coast. I hated deceiving my husband and I had to say that I was away with my girlfriends.

The feelings of guilt took some of the oxygen away from our relationship, but when you are in love – with passion comes forgetfulness. Positano was magical and when I returned home to Rome I think my husband first began to sense a change in me. Sven and I were like two lost people. We had stolen time and now we could not avoid what had been born in our time together. Looking back over the years, I believe our destiny had already been decided. We were in a crisis period when we could not be together, but neither could we be without each other. I will always love June because it was the month that we first knew we were really in love.

I was never happy with subterfuge. Some days I would go to walk by the Tiber just to clear my head. Loving two people in different ways is such a painful experience. I remembered an old proverb that says that people in love are like bees: they leave their stings in one another. Silly songs go round in your head, corny songs you never noticed before with lyrics like 'torn between two lovers, feeling like a fool' or just simply 'torn'. How could we continue to meet and how could we be sure we would not be discovered? Only illicit lovers know this agony. Strained telephone calls, secret assignations you never feel relaxed with, only add to the frustration. Some may think this brings a frisson of excitement to life, but for me the need to reconcile my true feelings with my relationships was uppermost. I wanted love in the open.

The first time my husband invited Sven for a cruise aboard

the *Nancy One* was a painful experience. I found it difficult being in the same place with the two men I loved. No one knew anything, but I couldn't help but feel self-conscious. Seeing Sven there, so close but untouchable, was even worse. As my husband was very busy that summer, I knew he would not mind if I said I was taking a brief boat trip with my girl-friends. I cannot blame our love for the sweet deceit, but the experience was addictive and putting out roots.

With June came the World Cup – France 98 – and with it an invitation from Sven to a group including Giancarlo and me to come to Sweden for a long weekend. This was an offer my husband felt he could not refuse and actually welcomed. The trip would be my first time in Sweden and Sven wanted to make us feel like royalty. It started well – there were flowers in the car for me and chilled champagne. In Stockholm we were guests at the Grand Hotel opposite the Grand Palace, the royal residence of the kings and queens of Sweden. Our romance was still young enough for Sven to want to make a big impression on both me and my husband; he had enjoyed our hospitality in Rome on many occasions. Impressing me was the idea, and this holiday was his tour de force.

The itinerary for the visit was set up as a surprise party. The first event was a hot-air balloon flight, but the June weather turned cold and the trip had to be cancelled. As the next treat, Sven had organized a cruise in the archipelago around Stockholm, and had hired an old traditional boat with a Nordic captain to take us to the islands. In particular, he had heard about a very remote island with an old village of fishermen's huts that he wanted us to see. This outdoors, back-to-nature activity is a very Scandinavian idea of a holiday!

Sweden in summer is a land of perpetual light and, as we cruised further and further from our home port and day turned to evening, we began to get a sense of a neverending voyage, with a barbecue at the end that we might be too tired to eat. We were hoping to be back to watch the World Cup on television. The Viking captain seemed merry enough as he took an occasional nip from some local liqueur. We hoped he knew where he was going. Eventually, the island came into view and we could see a collection of huts clustered around what appeared to be a lagoon or, more ominously, a swamp. Land at last, we thought. With the boat now moored safely alongside the wooden jetty, we jumped off to stretch our legs.

Suddenly, a shadow swept across the pale sun and the sky darkened, as if night was falling. There was a high-pitched whining sound that grew in intensity as if the sky was filled with radio-controlled model aeroplanes. I have never seen such monster mosquitoes in my life – not even in Africa. I felt like Tippi Hedren (another Scandinavian) in the Hitchcock movie *The Birds* – but these were worse than the birds! Sven's day out was really starting to impress me. We made a run for the huts in the hope that we might get some respite. When we stumbled inside we discovered the insect netting was torn and the monsters were on the inside.

'I think we have all had enough now,' I said. 'Please Sven, can we go back to the hotel?'

Sven disappeared in a cloud of mosquitoes back to the boat and when he returned he had a sheepish grin that told me something was wrong.

'I am very sorry, but we can't go anywhere tonight,' he said.

'Why not?' I asked.

'Oh, it's the captain – the captain is drunk,' he replied with an incredulous look. I was halfway between laughter and tears.

My husband said perhaps we should be going back to the boat to try to get some sleep. I grabbed a blanket as Giancarlo and I headed back, hoping to find shelter in the cabin from insect hell – but someone had left the cabin door open and the monster insects were there too. Giancarlo dozed off, but the incessant whining made it quite impossible for me to sleep. I opened the cabin door and noticed a light on in Sven's hut. Gathering my blanket around me, I ran the gauntlet towards his door. When I crashed in I saw him sitting at the table with a friend, having a quiet drink. They both looked up smiling.

'Do you think this is funny – some sort of Scandinavian joke?' I said. 'I am allergic to mosquito bites and I'm swelling up everywhere. When we get back I am going to need a cortisone injection.' Then I picked up a glass of water from the table and adopted a threatening pose. 'Did you do this on purpose?'

Sven was completely taken by surprise. 'No, no,' he said. 'I didn't know.'

As I pretended to throw the water at him, I could not restrain myself and burst out laughing. We all fell about with the giggles. His friend left to try to rouse the captain and we were left alone with the mosquitoes.

'A lagoon filled with man-eating mosquitoes is not exactly the greatest setting for a love island,' I teased. 'I am going back to the boat and I'm going to lock myself in the bathroom – the one without a window.' Even in the bathroom, sleep evaded me.

By 5 a.m. the weary band had assembled and the captain, nursing a bad hangover, finally got us under way. Stockholm was three hours' cruising, but at least we had escaped the island of the man-eating mosquitoes. When we finally reached port and made our way back to the Grand, I could not wait to get into the shower and apply a full tube of anti-histamine cream to my swollen hands and face.

This was my welcome to Sweden – and one I will never forget. Since then, I always try to take a very active role in planning away dates with Sven, as otherwise you never know quite what to expect.

My husband and I returned to Rome and a week later we were invited to spend the weekend with friends in Monte Carlo. Shortly after, I received a call from Sven to say he would love to see me if I could get away. He was in France for the World Cup and thought we could snatch a few days in St

Tropez before the weekend. Again, I played the girlfriend card to allow me to slip away to France. As I look back now, it all seems so crazy and unreal.

St Tropez was a turning point in our relationship. As a last-minute decision, we decided to attend a World Cup match in Marseilles. The stakes were high as we mingled invisibly with the crowd to watch the game. The match was the semi-final between Holland and Brazil, and Brazil won, but Sven and I were on a different planet as we watched the match hand in hand. This was the first time we went to a game together and the wonderful realization we had was that nobody knew about it. Things would never be the same again. I think we both knew we could not maintain the deception much longer. Sven would soon be away with the team to prepare for the season and I would be going on holiday with my husband for a few weeks in Sardinia and on the boat in Greece. We would have little chance to see each other – it would be the longest period apart since we met.

When you are crazy in love, being apart is a form of emotional starvation. You can't eat, you can't sleep and you can't do anything except think about the one you want to be with. Being on holiday with my husband in this mood was very hard. Giancarlo was so considerate and rational. I felt my pettiness and irritation were churlish. He noticed my moods and was worried by my change of character, but I don't think he ever suspected an affair. That made it all the more difficult. Sven was also undergoing duress and we were both plotting to find a way to spend more time together. The answer came whilst we were in Sardinia in the form of the arrival in the harbour of the grand boat belonging to Sergio Cragnotti, the owner of Lazio. There was to be a party on board. We were invited and Sven would also be there.

Sven had booked into the same hotel on the Costa Esmeralda in the hope that we could find some private time together and in the end I was able to steal away for a few precious hours. We were both exhausted with the stress of our unhappy situation when we met. I could see his face was white and drawn with anxiety.

'What is the matter?' I asked, concerned at first that there was some problem with the team.

'It's us,' he said. 'I cannot bear the situation any more and I want us to be together. I want you to leave your husband.' The long separation had made us realize that we couldn't live without each other. 'We can't go on like this,' he said, 'we have to give ourselves a deadline. When you return from your holiday on the boat at the end of the summer, you have to tell him or we are finished.'

I had loathed the subterfuge and I hated living a lie in the face of the other man I loved. We had come to a crisis of discontent through the long summer of love restrained. Now there was no way out without telling my husband and causing him intense suffering. But Sven and I were also in pain, and I could not bear the thought of losing him.

My husband and I returned to Rome in mid-September.

Despite Sven's plea to make a decision, I needed more time. In a way I had already made the decision in Sardinia and in my quiet moments of contemplation on the boat. But I couldn't bear to hurt Giancarlo. After so many years with a man I respected and loved, and who had done nothing but cherish me, to wound him in such a way was a crushing choice to make. And yet I could not live with the deceit involved in being unfaithful. It is not in my nature and I found the whole situation impossible. I kept thinking of the legend of King Arthur, whose queen, Guinevere, fell in love with Sir Lancelot. I felt we were a trapped triangle. I knew both men loved me and that only I could make the choice.

As I hesitated, Sven and I had endless, agonizing telephone conversations during which the threat of having to finish was repeated. I knew I needed to confront the situation and act. Sven could not wait for ever – I don't think he would allow his love life to begin to affect his professional concentration. Sergio Cragnotti had spent a fortune buying new players and Sven was expected to make a difference with his new men. The forthcoming season was vital for him. Then, as each day I kept trying to postpone what had to be done, Sven made an extraordinary decision. He offered to come with me to break the news to my husband so that he could help and support me through the trauma. After all, all we had done was fall in love. This was the price we had to pay. I think I loved him most at that moment for his conviction that he should do the right thing. I found this unique in a man; I had never encountered this attitude before, so reminiscent of the eighteenth- or nineteenth-century codes of honour that sometimes ended in a duel. Sven had shown extraordinary strength and determination of spirit to win me. He also felt a sense of responsibility towards my husband as a friend.

The date we broke the devastating news to my husband was Saturday, 25 September 1998. I will remember the day until I die. Giancarlo knew that Sven wanted a meeting with him and had suggested that he come over before lunch on that Saturday. I just couldn't bring myself to face up to the encounter, so we decided I would try to tell him the day before, on Friday 24th, ahead of Sven's meeting. But then I changed my mind again at the last minute. Instead I went to the movies with friends. Of course, I couldn't concentrate on the movie. I was filled with a terrible dread of what was to come the following morning.

When Sven arrived that Saturday, I was upstairs in our penthouse. It was a bright September day and, as I looked down from the balcony, I could see Giancarlo and Sven sitting on the terrace. My husband was wearing his sunglasses. He looked up and called me to come down, saying he was going to open a bottle of champagne to start the weekend. I knew there was nowhere to hide and I could not cancel this showdown any more. I walked to the stairs and began to make what felt like the longest descent of my life. The set was Sven stage right, my husband stage left; I entered centre stage and headed for the couch between them.

Giancarlo thought that Sven had come over to talk about business or a private matter and I heard him ask, 'You don't mind Nancy being here?'

Sven said, 'No, not at all – what I have to say concerns you both.' I just wanted the floor to open.

Sven started to lead the conversation and hesitated for what seemed like an eternity. It was obviously very difficult for him to speak. Finally, he told Giancarlo that he had fallen in love with me and that he had never meant this to happen. As he spoke I watched my husband. And all that I could see was his sunglasses.

Neither of us could read my husband's reaction behind the sunglasses. He was very calm. He looked at Sven and said, 'Well Sven, I have heard your side of the story. Now I want to hear what Nancy has to say.' He turned to me with his dignified manner that I loved so much and said, 'Nancy, is this true?'

I was lost again, desperate to reassure Sven but also not to hurt my husband. 'Yes, I think so,' I said. 'What he is saying is true.'

I saw both men tense and I knew my answer had satisfied no one. My husband heard hesitation in my answer and interpreted it as there being the possibility of some hope for us. For Sven, although he had heard my 'Yes', the hesitation gave him a nagging doubt about my resolve.

My husband was still cold as ice behind his sunglasses. I couldn't see his eyes and that made the tension worse. Then he got up and said in a very controlled voice, 'OK Sven, now you have to go. You have a match to prepare for and I need to speak with Nancy. We have the weekend. I suggest we talk on Monday.'

Sven looked dumbstruck. I knew he was expecting me to go with him, riding off into the sunset like the ending of a romantic movie. Instead the whole thing was a dreadful anti-climax. I knew that he wanted to protest. His face was wracked with emotion and I could see the white heat of shock and frustration boiling up. I knew I had to get him out of the house.

'You have to go now and leave me to deal with this,' I said. 'Now I have to deal with the consequences. You can't just throw me across the saddle of your charger and carry me off.' I was in tears. I loved both men and both loved me, and that is what made it so difficult and so complicated. Sven turned on his heel and left without a word. My husband left shortly after to go for a drive and a walk to clear his head. I waited in the house. When he returned we tried to talk, but he did not want to accept the situation. He said we should go slowly. Perhaps he had expected that something like this might happen because of our difference in age. This was the start of his battle to win me back.

Over dinner he tried again, saying, 'I don't think you are ready to leave this house.' He warned me that this may be just an infatuation and that I should think of the consequences. The atmosphere changed when I told him that I had planned to go to Sven's away match against Perugia the next day, Sunday. Giancarlo was not happy, as he had thought he would have the weekend to try to work things out. Out of desperation, he told me to be very careful as any action might be used against me if things went legal. I told him that although I had stayed with him, I had to be fair to Sven as well: I had to go to the game, but I would be back in the evening.

I went to the match with my special friend Lia. She had offered to accompany me when I had called her, feeling desperate and sure that I couldn't go alone. She was such a comfort. We sat in the director's box and I found myself next to the Chairman. This was the first of Sven's matches that I would attend publicly as his guest. I knew that seeing me there made him happy. It was a declaration of intent. He was not so happy when we met at his house later and I told him that I would have to return to my husband that night. He asked me to stay, and I wanted to, but my husband had begged me to come back and was expecting me. When I arrived home, I found Giancarlo very upset but happy that I was back. I think that gave him false hope.

After the holidays my husband had to go back to work and I had to make a decision. Sven wanted me to up everything and move in with him and could not see what was holding me back. But it was not that easy. I had to pack up all my personal things, including my head and my heart, and sort out my domestic arrangements. My husband did not want me to leave and did not accept how serious things were. I was going to need time in a neutral space to sort out my feelings. I don't think either man liked my decision to move into the Lord Byron Hotel but for both of them it was the lesser of two evils.

The Lord Byron is a small family hotel with period decor close to the Villa Borghese, not far from the top of the Spanish Steps and the house of John Keats. Named after the English lord, poet and adventurer, the hotel is one of the most discreet in Rome. Better still, I knew the manager and it was close to home. Sven was not happy with this period of adjustment and the need for legal separation. Whereas I tend to say what I think in the heat of the moment, Sven will brood and keep things within, simmering away. But I am an independent spirit and eventually even he had to accept that I wanted to do things my way. Over the two months of legal separation I became a gypsy again and put all my belongings in storage. This entailed many trips to the house with my indispensable Mona, who had kept house for me for the past five years, when my husband was out to gather up my stuff. Sven and I also went back and forth between the hotel and his house to be together.

During this time I lived I got to know more of the staff and people behind the scenes at Lazio. In particular, Sven introduced me to the bishop who held the official team mass every week. He was also the chaplain of the prison in Rome and the more we talked, the more interested in his work I became and I wanted to get involved in his plans for English classes and special visits for inmates. Soon, he became something of a spiritual mentor to me. It was certainly a surprise when one day he offered to take Sven and me on a tour of the Pope's private apartments. Of course we went and he also showed us the recently restored Sistine chapel. It was so strange and almost overpowering to be in there without the usual crowds of tourists. I returned to the Vatican the following year in 2000 when Lazio won the Scudetto. Sergio Cragnotti had arranged for a private reception with the Pope for the players, some of the staff and their families. Although he was so frail he radiated an immense sense of the sublime. I could hardly believe that this venerable father of the church had been a keen football player as a young man in his native Poland. It was such a great honour to be able to speak with him and receive his blessing.

So began my introduction to the new world of football. It was exciting to be part of Sven's world and to explore a dimension very different from anything I had known. I had to learn a completely new routine, with training in the morning and training in the afternoon. If you are the partner of a manager, you have to arrange your schedule around his – that is if you want the relationship to work. At the weekends, when our relationship was still private, I was a real football widow. The weekends can be a lonely time for the partners of all the men involved in football. It took time for me to adjust to organizing my weekends alone.

After I had spent two months at the Lord Byron, Sven and I decided to look for a house together. In the meantime, I moved to his villa in the hills close to the Vatican walls. Sven was away with the team on Saturdays and Sundays and I could not be with him, as we were trying to stay out of the public eye. To cheer me up, he always sent me flowers on Saturdays. All my clothes had been in storage for months and I was back living out of a suitcase. To make matters worse, I was still under pressure from my husband to return and the weekend was usually the time he would choose to ring me.

Moving in together seemed to coincide with a resurgence for Lazio. On 6 December they defeated the champions, Juventus, and went on to a string of nine victories in a row. Suddenly the star team was back on top and could do no wrong. The Italian media, second only to the English media, were all over Sven: it was inevitable that our cover would be blown before long. I think Sven was tired of hiding me from the public. One night we were dining in the footballers' favourite after-match paparazzi restaurant, Celestina ai Parioli, the best pizza place in town, when the story broke. I had tried not to hurt my husband for as long as possible, but we could not remain undiscovered for ever. As shock waves reverberated around Roman society, we were the talk of the town for several weeks. An official separation was granted and, at last, Sven and I were free to be together and I began to go to matches openly. But my husband still hoped to win me back.

Sven wanted me to get divorced as soon as possible. In Italy it takes three years to get divorce proceedings finalized.

Giancarlo and I were married in New York, however, and there you can in some circumstances obtain a 'quickie' divorce in almost half the time. Sven wanted me to press Giancarlo for this. Then I had word that my husband had been admitted to hospital for cardiac tests as his heart rhythms were fluctuating. Naturally, I felt both worried and guilty. There is no doubt that he was ill from the stress but, knowing me well, he knew he could play on my sympathy for him to try to get me back. What I did not know was that he had asked for a private meeting with Sven and, behind my back, the two fine gentlemen had come to an arrangement on how to proceed. Giancarlo was playing his last card and Sven had to concede, but I was blind to it. This honour-code acceptance of each other was getting us closer to a King Arthur–Queen Guinevere–valiant Sir Lancelot triangle by the day.

Under pressure from Giancarlo, my family and my conscience, I was persuaded to move back into my husband's house. I could not understand why Sven, who was usually so adamant about my staying with him, was not trying to stop me. Why was he not fighting for me at a vulnerable moment? What I did not know was that my course had been set when Giancarlo planted the seed of doubt in Sven's mind by telling him to keep a watch on me and that I had said that I was not sure of my relationship with him. Later, when I knew the story, I did not blame my husband: he was only fighting for the woman he loved. But at the time I did blame Sven for not telling me or saying no to Giancarlo when they met secretly.

Instead I returned to Giancarlo's house at my most vulnerable. I had terrible nightmares that took me back to the coma. Since then I have had trouble sleeping without pills. I hated sleeping like strangers in the same house and knowing that I would not be waking up with the man I loved. I had to end it.

Christmas was approaching, but for me this was not the season of good cheer. I felt trapped – a prisoner in a house that I had once loved, with all my memories of my marriage turning into ashes before my eyes. I believe that you can definitely die of a broken heart and the depression welling up inside me was far beyond separation anxiety. A few days before Christmas I knew that moving back had been a mistake. Neither the pain I would cause Giancarlo nor my parents' anger was going to hold me there. I fled back to Sven.

Sven had plans to return to Sweden for Christmas to be with his family. We decided to go together to get away from Italy and the feeling of despair. I will not forget standing in the check-in line and taking calls from my father and then from my husband. It was a bitter moment. My parents told me that if I went to Sweden not to call them over Christmas. I learned then that if you truly love, you have to pay the price of love and the value of the currency is measured in emotional pain. I was feeling very fragile and Sven was very tender, although he still kept hidden the pact he had struck with Giancarlo.

This would be my first Christmas in Sweden. It was 23 December and the day already seemed prematurely dark when we landed. Snow was falling as we headed off to spend Christmas with Sven's family. A new world full of doubts opened up. This was just a short break, as training commitments began in the New Year. While I was in Sweden I had news that my husband had been in and out of hospital over Christmas and I was full of guilt. A realization of how difficult this was for both of us became clearer than ever. I could not understand why Sven was so insecure in my love for him. Guilt can damage even the strongest relationship. On our way back to Rome, I told him that I must see my husband again and convince him that it was over. Sven could not understand this. He said if I was going back I should go back right away and he took me to my husband's house direct from the airport.

This was one of the worst times in my life and, as we drove across town, we were both crying. How could I make Sven understand that I was trying to find release from guilt? I had my whole Italian world standing against us and he – who should be my champion – was acting as if I had betrayed him. Another of my close friends, Wanna came with me to my husband's house to give me support over the New Year. To aid his recuperation and help me adjust, Giancarlo had organized a trip to the Swiss Alps for us. This was my saddest New Year's Eve ever. Sven wouldn't speak to me for days and I was pining for lost love. I think my husband realized for the first time that I really loved Sven and that this was a war he could not win. Then he was suddenly taken ill again and admitted to hospital. Then, when he was released the next day, we went back to Rome and I knew I would have to see Sven as soon as possible. I thought the battle with Sven must be over, but he was still feeling hurt and found it hard to understand my predicament. We had reached an impasse and our passion was blocked by his inability to trust in my love for him. I had given up so much and he did not seem prepared to wait for me to resolve my dilemma.

When I feel the world is against me, I travel. So I took off on my own and left my men to their own devices. I went to New York, then to Greece, then looked up old friends in Israel. My husband was relieved as he still felt he had a chance. Sven still sulked, unable to trust unreservedly the person who loved him the most. When I returned to Rome, Giancarlo had gone back into hospital for a last operation. Sven still seemed distant, although I knew he was in as much pain as I was. My husband proposed a business trip to New York that coincided with Valentine's Day. I expected Sven to object and I was very sad when he acquiesced and even told me that it was my choice. Of course he was right that it was my choice, but I couldn't understand why he didn't speak out.

On the flight I was overwhelmed by the claustrophobia of the whole situation, and then my husband began to play mind games with me. He said, 'Why didn't Sven try to stop you coming? He can't really care that much about you if he was prepared to let you go.'

'What do you mean he was prepared to let me go?' Sensing by his tone that there was something he wasn't telling me, I asked him what was going on between the two of them – had he been talking to Sven?

'Oh we have been talking together since last September,' he responded.

'What fine gentlemen – talking about me behind my back!' I asked him what they had talked about. Then I saw my husband look away as if I had touched a nerve.

'We just said that it was right to let you make your choice and make up your own mind.'

I could feel my hot temper rising. 'But Giancarlo, you know that I have made my choice. It is over between us and has been for months. We are in a legal separation and you are talking to Sven as if there is still something to decide.'

Suddenly, I saw it all. My husband had used my compassion for him and his illness to undermine Sven's trust in my love for him. He had planted a seed of doubt in Sven's mind, as if I had not fully made up my mind. 'Right,' I said, 'you are going to tell me everything.' I was full of disappointment, rage and bewilderment.

He could see that I was about to lose it. I think he knew the game was up. 'Well, Sven and I reached an agreement that we had to let you choose between us without any interference from either of us.' Giancarlo had been very clever. Over the last five months he had effectively manipulated both Sven and me into this hopeless position. I knew that he would go to any length to try to keep me, but for Sven to go along with it and reach an agreement – that was madness. No wonder he had been so moody, resentful and withdrawn. This was too much.

'OK! So let me understand this. You two reach an agreement – you make some sort of pact behind my back for me to choose between you when you both know my decision has already been made. This is crazy. Get on the phone right now and speak to Sven! And get me on the first plane back when we touch down.'

Giancarlo knew then that it was all over. He rang Sven and told him that he had had to confess the terms of their 'arrangement' and that I was angry with both of them. He also told Sven that I would be back to Rome the following day. Only men could cook up such a mad scheme to compound everyone's suffering and unhappiness. Now I knew why Sven had been acting so strangely and suffering like crazy.

The drama, however, was not yet over. The morning after our arrival in New York we were just walking past the Met when my husband received a phone call. I watched his face change and he became very upset: he had just been told that his sister-in-law had committed suicide. She had been suffering from cancer for some time and in a moment of despair had taken her own life. My husband took this very personally, as if fate was conspiring against him. Instead of staying in New York he decided to cut short his visit and we flew back to Rome together. All my plans for an airport dash to confront Sven had to be put on hold as, with mounting family pressure, I felt it was the right thing to support Giancarlo for the funeral and I wanted to pay my own respects to Bianca as I had seen the terrible things she had been through. After that I would make the changes.

My mood was sombre when I told Giancarlo I was leaving and that this time it was for ever. I did not look back as I left, knowing his pain was almost unbearable. At least Sven and I had each other.

Despite the pain we had caused each other, I could not help but admire my husband's fighting spirit and his determination to go to any lengths to win me back. On the other hand, it did not feel to me as though Sven was showing the same strength as when he had faced my husband at the outset. My Sir Lancelot had given in to doubts about his Guinevere, and instead of riding in on his charger and carrying me off had held back and sulked. The emotional pain of the break-up of my marriage was something we had to face. The rest was all imagination and issues of male pride. Love has its own rules, but both men had put me and themselves through a time of suffering unlike any other that I can remember.

Inevitably, by the time Sven and I were able to be together, my anger had cooled and all the frustration of the past months melted into joy. Sven told me he had accepted the arrangement with Giancarlo as he also had to take some responsibility for breaking up my marriage. The seed of doubt – that I might go back and that I might not love him – had been planted and he had given in to his own worst fears. Sven likes to avoid confrontation and he is always the gentleman – Gentleman Sven, I used to call him, and he is. I told him that he should have trusted our love and been more secure in the knowledge of my feelings for him. Underneath the cool exterior, he is very sensitive and only shows his true emotion when he feels certain of unconditional love. I expected him to be more understanding about my need to manage the break-up of my marriage and my family circumstances, but he had played right into my husband's fight-back plans and for a time we had both almost lost faith in each other.

We had reached a turning point in our relationship. Deciding to give myself to Sven was only the beginning of the process. You only discover love by being in love. You can't catch hold of it, as it always slips through your fingers. For us the bud had opened though the fruit was not yet on the tree. But a new phase had begun. From the moment we were together, Sven and I considered ourselves engaged. You do not leave a husband for anything less. For the Christmas of 1999, he gave me a beautiful diamond engagement ring.

By March 1999 Lazio were top of the League and Sven and I were happy to be out in the open. Once I began to attend matches in public and the press picked up on the success of Sven's high-flying team they began to associate me with that success. The media always likes a love story and, although it must have been torture for my ex-husband, they could not leave it alone. We laughed over the silliness of newspapers reporting the fans' desire to build a monument to me and that the language of love was making Sven communicate better with his players. This was all very flattering, but I also knew the fickleness of the Italian press. It could swing the other way if the team started to lose. At the end of April we were still League leaders and seven points clear of Milan with eight games to play. The Scudetto was within Sven's grasp and we were the toast of the town.

Now that Giancarlo had accepted the separation and my family was growing used to the new relationship, we could begin to live a more normal life. We finally found an apartment in Rome that would give us a new sense of life. The place I found was to die for; I have never known another like it. The historic building was situated on the Via del Corso and the penthouse apartment overlooked the Piazza del Popolo. In particular, the roof terrace had a 180-degree view of old Rome. It was the ideal choice for our honeymoon home. At the time, I never really thought about the practicalities for Sven or that a residence in such a public area might pose difficulties. In those days, Sven drove himself, and no private cars were allowed in the area. Parking was also a problem. Furthermore, he could hardly walk 100 paces without somebody flagging him. At that time I did not understand; now I do. Then I could think only of my bedroom attached to the cupola of Santa Maria degli Angeli. At that time, Sven would have done anything I asked to please me. I could not have been happier.

At the end of the season, things were very tense. Milan and

Lazio were racing neck and neck, with Lazio behind by one point on the last day. I was praying that Lazio would beat Parma and Milan would go down to Perugia. This would win us the League. Unfortunately, Milan won the coveted Scudetto by a single point. Even the press commented ironically that Milan had won Lazio's title. Of course Sven was down, but he still had his eyes on the European Cup. I began to go to most big matches.

My first experience of an English football stadium was Villa Park in Birmingham for the final of the European Cupwinners' Cup. I was on the edge of my seat for eighty long minutes with the game wide open until Lazio's spectacular goal won the match. After the disappointment of losing the UEFA Cup the previous year to Milan, and then giving away the Scudetto, winning Lazio's first European trophy was no small consolation for Sven. We could celebrate a famous victory and a new phase of our life together.

WINNING IN LOVE

●

Love makes bitter things sweet;
Love converts base copper into gold.
By love the pool is made clear;
By love pain is healed
By love the dead are brought to life,
By love a King is made a slave.

JALLAL AL-DIN RUMI

VIII

SVEN AND I HAVE ALWAYS BEEN SUN-WORSHIPPERS. We adore being by the sea soaking up the rays and, although we loved our penthouse in Rome (well I certainly did, although I'm not so sure about Sven), we liked to slip away to the beach whenever we could. There is a lovers' beach at Fregene, at the *villagio dei pescatori* (fishermen's village) that we used to drive out to if we wanted to escape the hustle of the city. Fregene is about 30 kilometres from the centre of Rome and is relatively unspoiled. It is still a working village and, if you walk along the beach, you can see the boats drawn up and the fishermen mending their nets. In the 1950s and 1960s the village had become famous as a kind of seaside artists' colony and many writers and film directors gravitated to the area for creative stimulation. Hollywood stars like Frank Sinatra and Dean Martin were regular visitors, and residents included such luminaries as

Alberto Moravia, Francesco Rossi, Pasolini, Fellini, Mastroianni and many others. There is also a fabulous local restaurant owned by the four Mastino brothers – called Mastino's, of course – where, in the family ambience, you can select freshly caught fish and just lose yourself in the moment. We began to spend more and more of our leisure time there and it was only natural to start thinking of acquiring a beach-side property of our own in this lovely spot.

We could not help falling in love and our emotional bond was so strong that, like a tsunami, it swept away everything in its path to change for ever all our existing relationships. Our love story, like birth, had begun painfully, and after such a dramatic year, we felt we needed to go a little further away to soothe and heal our souls. The answer was Polynesia and the enchanted islands of the Pacific Ocean. Part of our reason for the time away was to work things out. I was still smarting from the pain of Sven's cold withdrawal during the break-up of my marriage and his loss of trust in our love when he knew I had issues to resolve with my husband. He also needed time to come to terms with his feelings and the fear of loss of self-control that had made him react against me in such a way. The flood of passion had ushered in forgiveness, but we had not worked out all these feelings consciously and were still holding back from each other. Polynesia was a time of renewal; we discovered a new trust in each other that went beyond mere passion.

Sven and I had taken a sea chalet at Fregene on a rental basis. Houses on the sea park were like gold dust because it was under state ownership and protected by the Department of Environment of Rome. One day, I received good local intelligence – from the Mastino brothers – that a lady wanted to sell her chalet there. We did not hesitate and, once we had bought and secured our foothold, began to renovate. This was my baby, and I called in my brother, Jerome – by now a very talented architect – to take on remedial works with me for a design and development project. I love interior decoration and put my heart and soul into transforming the run-down property. By a stroke of luck, we were shortly able to acquire a second chalet immediately behind us and Jerome created a stunning design to link the two buildings into a wonderful (at least for us) architectural space. During our first summer there, Sven had been away with the team for the pre-season preparation. When he returned, I liked to distract him from football pressures with an inspection of all the works in progress on our house. I remember an amusing story that sums up my man. I had been working on the garden and the terrace, setting out some benches and chairs for dinner parties and entertaining outside, when he arrived and began to count up the number of seats. When he reached twenty he turned to me and said, 'Do I take it you intend to invite twenty people here every night?' He has always been allergic to large social gatherings; he prefers to meet in small groups and is quite reserved. I really have to push him to entertain. Sven's perfect number is two; four is a party and six is a crowd!

This house became a refuge for Sven and me. Our

penthouse in Rome was in the most fabulous location; but the practical drawbacks for Sven were becoming more apparent. The biggest problem was that it was so central and, therefore, lacked any kind of privacy; he could hardly walk 50 metres without being stopped. Fregene was our hideaway house and the place where I have shared some of the happiest moments of my life with Sven. I have my guardian angel over the fireplace and a favourite Belgian chandelier above the table; the walls are hung with my best works of art – paintings by De Chirico and Balla, and my favourite paintings in sand. Two lovely ladies, Nadia and Luisa, take it in turns to keep an eye on the house to this day and, every time I leave this special place, I feel as if I am committing some kind of sin.

That summer brought another surprise. I fell pregnant for a third time. Sven and I had not set out to have a child, even though I think that Sven liked the idea. We were just letting things happen and then, suddenly, I missed a period. Although the timing was not ideal, on this occasion I felt different: I wanted a child. Sven was away and I did not tell him immediately as I wanted to be sure before raising his expectations. When I went for a check-up my doctor told me I was almost two months gone and, given my history, advised me to take life a bit easy. Sadly, once again it was not to be. The miscarriage happened whilst Sven was still away and I found myself having to cope with the crisis alone. When I told him, I think we were both in shock. This time I felt much more physically violated by the death of the new life within me before it had had a chance to grow. It was a far more devastating experience for me than anything before, not only because of what we had endured but because Sven was the love of my life. I was a strong and healthy young woman and my physical recovery was fast, but the scars still remain deep inside. It had all happened so fast, with the realization of my being pregnant coming only a short time before the miscarriage. But I believe Nature must take her course.

Sven and I suffered all the trauma of bereavement. We both yearned after what we had lost, even though we knew it was not an ideal time to have a child. Behind those famous glasses of Sven's there is a very kind and sensitive man and we became even closer through sharing this experience. I think the realization that our relationship had had a physical consequence gave us the impetus to let go and give in to love. In acknowledging and understanding how much we had endured together, our relationship came of age. After my earlier termination and miscarriage, and now a second miscarriage, I had to consider the possibility that it might not happen for us. Although I love children, I have never wanted a child so much that I would consider IVF. It's never been the right time. I believe that what is to be will be. I don't know where my life will take me. Maybe at some point I would be happy to give love to an adopted child. After all, a child is born as much in the heart as in the body. We will see what happens.

After the summer, Sven immersed himself in football once

again. The same developments that took place in England with the Premier League in the early 1990s had also taken place in Italy. The top clubs had signed up for lucrative new television rights deals with the emerging digital stations and Lazio had also taken advantage of the expanded Champions League money-go-round. As we have seen, Sergio Cragnotti had purchased more players and Sven was building up a star-quality Lazio squad that he was determined would win the Scudetto. He started well, lifting the European Super Cup from Manchester United in Monaco before the domestic season had started. This was a very special game for me, sitting in the Royal Box close to Prince Albert and all the directors of Lazio. When the match ended in victory there was such elation that the Chairman led me on to the pitch to congratulate Sven and the players. It was so special to be together at the very moment of his triumph. The world seemed to contract to just the two of us while the crowd roared around us.

The season started with eight unbeaten games, taking Lazio one point clear of Juventus and three points ahead of Milan. Then, just as we thought things were going well, we suffered a humiliating whitewash against Roma. The result rocked the team and Sven could not hide his concern: this was not the performance he needed to win the Scudetto. I was fascinated by how fast things can change; a year in football is as long as it is in politics.

I don't think the public – even the fans – really stop to think about the pressure on football managers and players at the highest level. These few men are the focus for the hopes and fears of so many. Thanks to the power of television, football, as the great global game, has become the new international arena. Communities everywhere – hamlets and villages, towns and cities, regions and countries – all project their sense of identity on to their football club. To be responsible for so many expectations, and to be on the receiving end of such attention, is truly awesome. Who does not want to be Victor Ludorum – the winner of the games? But the thumbs can be only up or down; there is no halfway house. There is always a little of 'those about to die salute you' at the opening of a match ceremony, and, as managers know only too well, 'the King must die, long live the King' is always just a few bad results away. You cannot ever relax your guard.

Lazio was the only club still in the running for the treble crown: Serie A, the Italian Cup and the Champions League. Being in contention, however, is not good enough: you must win. The team's performance improved with a quarter-final victory over Juventus, then, in February, they triumphed over Venezia in the first-leg semi-final of the Italian Cup. Lazio were still on course for the Scudetto and the Cup. The slide began with a goalless draw against Parma and, worse, losing to the unrated Verona. Juventus were motoring and now nine points clear. No one thought Lazio could come back from so far behind except me and Sven. He just goes into quiet mode and broods, but underlying the brooding is a master tactician with a steely determination to win, as he moves players like chess pieces towards the optimum performance in his imagination.

Sven has always invited a close relationship with his players. This is not to say that he allows familiarity. He always keeps an unconscious distance, as he does with almost everybody. He does, however, believe in getting to know his men well. He may sit on the bench in matches and keep a quiet dignity that some mistake for a lack of passion, but he has a good rapport with his players. He can be quite stern but is always accessible. I have always been attracted to leaders and often, at matches, I have watched Sven, comparing him to a general – a Greek *strategos* rather than a Roman rabble rouser. He does not run around the touchline, but is a rather more elegant manager, lifting the game above its sometimes downmarket, laddish reputation. My ex-husband, in an unusually snobbish moment, said to me, 'So, Nancy, you are going to be reading the *Sporting News* now rather than the *Financial Times*,' meaning that life with a football manager was beneath me. I don't think so.

With pressure mounting, Sven knew that his top players were vital in bringing about a resurgence. If he was to get the show back on the road to win the Scudetto, he would have to rely on his core champions. These were the players that would make the difference.

When Sven first went to Roma in the early 1980s he was one of the youngest managers and couldn't speak Italian. He had to learn the ways of Italian football the hard way. At first he tried to ban *ritiro* – or 'time out', the practice of meeting at a hotel before the Sunday matches, but in the end he found that old habits die hard and had to reinstate the custom because it was good for team morale. Ever since he had learned this lesson, he had been looking for ways to enhance the team's psychological fitness. That season he put into practice for the first time an idea we had come up with together of a week's 'family get-together' so that the team could get to know each other on a personal level, which would enhance the bond between the players. Sven was the first to start the practice in Italy and we certainly found it the best way to break down barriers and build team spirit – the results spoke for themselves in terms of trophies. He also later introduced it in England and, although it caused some controversy at the time, the jury is still out on its benefit. I know the English can be very old-fashioned and hair-shirt about this sort of thing, and often adopt a 'no-pain, no-gain' approach. My feeling is that, when the pressure is on, the player bond may well prove decisive.

The next match was in England – the Champions League match against Chelsea. I decided to attend the match and, hopefully, fit in some shopping in London. Taking on Chelsea at home at Stamford Bridge is always a formidable challenge. They had not lost a single European match in over thirty games, and Sven knew that if he lost this one his job would be on the line. We all knew the supreme test would be mind over matter and indeed, after an agonizing match, Lazio won.

As if by magic, the energies changed and Lazio regained their form. Fate takes a hand in football, as it does in all things. As the drama played out on the pitch, it only served to confirm that life is stranger than fiction.

As football legends go, the story of Sven's lifting the Scudetto and Lazio's triumphant season beats many. Living it was one of the most extraordinary times of my life. Perhaps Sven's sweetest gift to me was the promise before the match that, if Lazio won, he would dedicate the Scudetto to me. I felt like a medieval princess giving her champion her favour. Both the final matches – Lazio versus Reggina, and Juventus versus Perugia at the Perugia stadium – took place on the same day. Lazio had only one aim and that was to win – and at half time they were winning. Meanwhile in Perugia, just after the close of the goalless first half, the heavens opened and a virtual typhoon engulfed the stadium. The pitch was flooded and, when the referee tested the pitch, the ball sank like the proverbial lead balloon into the mire. The referee, Pierluigi Collina, found himself in a very contentious position. The plan had been to synchronize the start of the second halves of both matches to avoid any accusations of foul play, but now in Perugia Collina stalled for time, whilst in Rome the resumption of the match was also delayed. The tension in the whole country was nerve-wracking.

After three-quarters of an hour, the referee in Rome decided play would have to resume. Sven turned round from the bench and gave me our secret sign. We had everything to play for. In the end Lazio scored again, ensuring that they were the winners. With the match in Rome over, the game began on the sodden pitch at Perugia. All of Italy stopped to catch the result. The second half had just begun when the miracle we were praying for happened: Perugia scored, winning the match and denying points to Juventus.

Italy went wild, and Sven and I were fêted about Rome. All his efforts had been vindicated – the Scudetto was ours.

After the match we attended the hurriedly organized victory dinner party at the sports centre at Formello, Lazio's home ground. I will never forget this as it was almost impossible to leave the stadium. Sven and I had to go back to our apartment, although we knew the Lazio fans gather in the Piazza del Popolo to celebrate. We were lucky to escape detection and I now really understood the problem with the location and had to admit Sven had been right all along.

The Scudetto was not the only title that Sven won in this great millennium year. He made the double, winning the Italian Cup. Unfortunately, his luck ran out for the triple crown and he had to concede the Champions League after defeat in the quarter-final to Valencia. I recall the wistful expression on his face when he came home very late that night – we stayed up together until dawn. The triple had just slipped through his fingers. Over his three years at Lazio, Sven won seven coveted trophies and went from being a successful coach to a star manager.

True to his promise, at the public ceremony to celebrate winning the League, Sven dedicated his victory to me. I think by this time I was more than a mascot for the team. Players, press and fans all knew of our code language. When I attended matches, I adopted the habit of sitting in the director's box behind the team bench. As a good luck charm, Sven would always turn to me, bow his head and make a sign with his hand. This was our little ritual.

I had grown to understand the football way of life. Win or lose, it takes a long time to get the adrenalin out of your system. Sleep is elusive, and the long nights need talking through. Sven and I would have a few drinks – champagne or Scotch. Maybe watch the replay. A late supper at 4 a.m.; a plate of pasta all washed down with Glenmorangie. Sometimes we would be having dinner when all normal people are having breakfast. Then, the day after the match, you do nothing. This can become an addictive life.

Now was the time for celebration. Lazio were on a high, Sven was top in town and we were happy in the knowledge that we would soon be able to get away on holiday. On the spur of the moment, I thought that it would be nice to throw a surprise party for Sven on the beachside at Fregene to cele-brate winning the Scudetto and the Italian Cup. Mastino's was an obvious choice. I would have everything catered by the brothers, with the sea as a magnificent backdrop. As it was holiday time, I had only a few days to arrange it all, so I solicited the help of Tord Grip, Sven's right-hand man, his wife Inga and a group of our closest friends. Everyone was sworn to strict secrecy. The thing that I have always liked about proper celebrations is fabulous fireworks. I wanted to have them for the party on the scale of Guy Fawkes Night or 4 July so that I could create a seascape spectacular that would make a real impression. That I most certainly did – but it was not quite the impression I was hoping for.

It was Saturday night and I had lulled Sven into thinking we were going to Mastino's for one of our usual quiet romantic seaside suppers. That was one of our favourite things to do. As we approached, the restaurant was more or less blacked out, although there were many more cars there than usual. Sven thought this was all a little mysterious but did not suspect anything unusual. I was like a little girl, bubbling up with all the excitement of preparing a big surprise for someone she loves.

As we entered, the lights went on and the big band struck up. I looked at Sven, expecting to see his face light up with joy at being surrounded by all his friends and colleagues. Instead he had gone white with shock. His eyes were wide and staring – and I knew, instantly, that his first reaction was searing anger and that my surprise party was the worst surprise he could have had. I was confused and hurt. I had only been trying to show appreciation for the man I loved, and all his friends and the people in our close circle had thought it was a wonderful idea. Standing in the spotlight before 150 people he had to grit his teeth, grin and bear it. He turned to me in disbelief, then he walked off to circulate. For the rest of the night I was subjected to torture by killer glance. Even the fireworks, which lasted for twenty minutes, were torment. Sven's face was just beginning to relax as the party ended. I thought everyone had had a fabulous time except the one person it had all been for. As he shook hands with the guests to say goodbye, I burst into tears.

Tord Grip came up and put his arms around me to give me comfort. 'A wonderful party – now it really feels like we have won,' he said. 'Don't worry about Sven. You know he is very self-conscious. He loves the spotlight but he hates it at the same time. You have nothing to be concerned about. I will talk to him.'

It was three in the morning when Sven came to see me to apologize. 'Nancy, I am very sorry. It was a very good party. I am not good with surprises – it was a shock.'

Of course, now I look back on it, I see that my own disappointment that the party was not quite the success with Sven I had hoped clouded my perception. I was just so mortified that he was not immediately delighted, that I saw black looks and anger where there weren't. Distracted by the stress and excitement of it all I couldn't see Sven getting his own quieter enjoyment at the party, but I was glad we were able to resolve it at the end of the night. We kissed and made up, but for me it opened up a new window on Sven's individuality and revealed the bubbling hot tub of unresolved personal issues within. I think we all like to be in control, some of us more than others, and for Sven the sudden feeling of being out of control was completely disorientating. For him, this experience was also an opportunity to observe his own fears. The great thing about our relationship is that when we make mistakes we can look at them honestly, learn from them and move on to new things together.

The summer of 2000 was a golden season as we basked in the warm glow that comes with success. We had been through two extraordinary years and now we decided that we should explore love again by taking a summer holiday. We decided to start with a spell in Sweden. We both love Scandinavia in the spring and summer. During the warmer months, with all the flowers in bloom, it looks so different from the snowbound images we usually associate with that part of the world. Sven and I did not have our own house in Sweden then, so we stayed with his parents. We both loved to walk and experience the joy of solitude. After this sojourn to the north, we decided to head for the Mediterranean to sail around the Greek islands on my boat, the *Nancy One*, which I had kept following my divorce from Giancarlo. To defray the expenditure and upkeep of the boat, Giancarlo and I had put the vessel out to charter with a Greek lady, Maria Mamos, who became a very close friend and confidante, and I continued this arrangement after my marriage ended. By working a charter system, the boat pays for herself and I can use her whenever I want – all I have to do is to book her out to myself. Sven enjoys spending time on the boat, but not to the extent that I do. A week is enough for him, whereas I feel completely at home on the sea and could live on board for ever. I love the Greek islands: Santorini, Mykonos, Samos and Patmos, the island where St John wrote his Revelation. My favourite group, and now Sven's too, is the Cyclades. That summer break we sailed around all these historic, mythical islands and they became very special to us. We call them the islands of love.

The new season started with a drive to build more player power. Sven's push for the remainder of 2000 was to win the Champions League. Lazio were primed and Sven believed that this was the strongest team he had managed in his career.

One day in early October, as we were having dinner, I could see from Sven's manner that he had something very important to tell me. He said that Athole Still, his agent, had called to say that the English Football Association wanted to open up a dialogue.

'Do you mean they want you to manage the national team?' I asked.

'Yes, it would seem so – the team has not being doing very well.'

I knew that Sven was about to renew his contract with Lazio and, having just built his ideal team, this would be a huge upheaval. 'Do you think it is the right time?' I asked.

'Well, there is never a right time but this is a once-in-a-lifetime opportunity,' he replied philosophically.

I think I knew then that destiny had already taken over, though Sven had not yet made any decision and there would be much soul-searching before he finally made his choice. There is no doubt in my mind that he viewed the chance to manage England as the climax of his career. For us mainland Europeans – although we hate to admit it – England has a special status in football. There is nowhere in the world with equal passion for the game. I began to think about London.

ENGLAND CALLING

●

No one regards what is before his feet;
We all gaze at the stars.

QUINTUS ENNIUS

IX OFTEN MOMENTOUS DECISIONS THAT HAVE affected the course of my life have been made when I have been far removed from the centre of the action. When Sven took his decision on the England manager's job, I was on the other side of the Atlantic, visiting New York to review my property portfolio after the long summer holiday. The week of my departure to America co-incided with the arrival of the private plane bringing Adam Crozier, England Football Association chief, and David Dein, Chairman of Arsenal, to Rome to discuss the Football Association proposals with Sergio Cragnotti and Sven. I was looking forward to meeting up with my brother Jerome in New York and catching up with old friends whilst attending to business. I had no idea of the media storm that was gathering and that my initiation to the extraordinary world of the English press would begin almost before Sven's signature was dry on the contract. England was changing my life even before I had arrived.

The offer from England had come as a complete surprise and we had both weighed up the pros and cons before I departed. No decision had been made other than that the whole matter should be kept entirely secret. Sven had a good relationship with Sergio Cragnotti; they had become close as they shared the glory of the most successful season in Lazio's history. Sven wanted to explore all his options, as there were a lot of considerations to take into account. From his perspective these management decisions were not so much about personal reward (although that was important) but about the ability to purchase players and build teams – the professional reward. He had given his vision for Lazio to his Chairman; now he would consider the proposals from England and give Cragnotti the chance to make a counter-offer. That would only be fair in the circumstances and it would help him make up his mind.

Back in the city of my birth, I had been very busy with my own affairs. This would be the last time that I would see the twin towers of the World Trade Center. I had just returned to my hotel after dinner with Jerome when Sven called to tell me about his meeting with Adam Crozier and David Dein. He was in a real dilemma, as the timing could not have been worse. Naturally, Lazio wanted Sven to finish the season – they were still in the Champions League and after their recent successes had everything to play for. Adam Crozier, meanwhile, would have liked Sven to take up the England job as soon as possible. Sven did not want just to abandon Lazio and his sense of loyalty led him to look for a compromise if he was going to leave. The deal he felt most comfortable with was to see his club through the season and start part-time with England from February, when they were due to play Spain at Villa Park. By doing this he hoped to accommodate both sides to his own best interest. As we talked over the options we were mindful of the pitfalls of that old proverb of trying to serve two masters. We did not expect our worst fears to be realized quite so soon.

After the meeting in Rome, the decision was made within twenty-four hours and the next time Sven called was to wake me up in the early hours of the morning with the simple words, 'I have signed.' The whole deal was top secret and we agreed that I would return to Rome as soon as possible. As I turned out the light to go back to sleep my imagination began to play and the prospect of what lay ahead kept me awake. I was in a half slumber when my mobile rang again. As I answered I heard an English voice saying, 'Nancy, I am from the *Daily Mail*. Would you like to comment on Sven's decision to take over the England national team?' This was my introduction to the English press.

I was amazed. How had they got my number and how did they know about a decision that was supposed to be top secret? I said, 'Do you know what time it is? It's five in the morning and I am sleeping – I don't know what you are talking about!' With that I put the phone down.

This was just the beginning. My hotel began receiving a string of strange calls asking to be put through to my room. Jerome and I booked tickets on Alitalia back to Rome. As I was settling into my seat, I noticed Jerome in conversation with the person in the next row. He was laughing when he turned to me and said, 'We have the pleasure of the company of the *Daily Mail*'s New York City bureau chief.' I was just amazed at both the audacity and the ingenuity – all in search of a scoop.

Sven's decision had been made quickly and when I rejoined him he was concerned to hear about my encounters with the English press before his decision had been announced formally. Sven is very dedicated to his work. As such he was thinking about the team welfare and his commitment to Lazio. He had wanted to keep a low profile and the prospect of the growing press attention in both Italy and the United Kingdom was very upsetting for him. Taking on England was a big challenge, but I knew that in his heart this was the only job for him. As the speed of events had overtaken us, neither of us had given much thought to how we would be perceived in England. We knew there would be some fierce criticism from the old guard both of Sven himself and of the Football Association's decision to appoint a foreign manager. Sven was not afraid of that. His greatest fear is not living up to the standards he sets for himself. I have to say that I felt very positive about the move: all my intuition told me that England had a very special place in my destiny.

The day chosen by the FA to present the new England manager to the British press was 2 November 1999. I will never forget it because after the announcement Sven had to make a morning dash to Luton airport to allow him to get back for the Lazio training session in the afternoon. Even for Sven, who has faced the international media in many different situations, a full assembly of the English press corps was a daunting prospect. My good friend and FA director of communications at the time, Paul Newman, told me later that Sven had met every question flung at him by playing the straight man, talking in the third person, answering the questions with questions, as if conferring, and saying as little as possible. If there was a question he did not wish to answer he could always play the English at their own game by assuming the mask of the Swedish 'Johnny Foreigner'. The result was he gave away very little. As the press came to learn later, this was not any premeditated media strategy but just Sven being Sven. This is his way.

In Italy, the football fraternity can be as conservative as in England but, although there were some calls for Sven to resign, there was little hostility over his decision to move to England. In fact, Cragnotti said that he saw nothing wrong with Sven being at a press conference in England in the morning and training at Formello in the afternoon. Indeed, a match was played on the same day as the confirmation of his appointment, and Sven was delighted to receive the applause of the fans as he took his seat. I felt proud of my man as Lazio were victorious on the night. Many people also felt that Italian football could take some credit for the fact that the first foreign manager to coach the England national team had made much of his superstar reputation in Italy.

Unfortunately, no sooner had the news of Sven's new appointment broken, than the team performance began to deteriorate and Lazio began a run of bad results. The fans are prepared to support you when you are winning, but it does not take much for the tide to turn. It looked as if fate was conspiring against the plan to please everyone. I knew Sven was questioning himself and the team, but one of his great qualities is to keep a cool head in a crisis. He had little time to think of England, but he was able to take comfort from the fact that Tord Grip, his 'eyes and ears' for spotting new talent, was already scouting from the touchline in the UK.

Sven was trying to understand what was going wrong and whether there was more to the adverse run of play than bad form and bad luck. He had his pick of players, but the team was not scoring goals. So much had happened over the year I couldn't wait for the Christmas holidays to escape the pressure and find time for us to be together to reflect on our options. The last match before Christmas was in my old university town of Bari and Lazio won this great game in style. Sven hoped the year-end high would be a return to form.

The end of the year held one more unfortunate surprise – an ugly incident of alleged racism between Patrick Viera and Sinisa Mihajlovic – that added to the pressure on Sven as he began seriously to consider his position at Lazio. At the beginning of our relationship I knew that Sven had been concerned about how the Lazio fans would react to me; I think he worried that some might say he was more concerned with his love life than his football. But as his success began to sweep all before him, I became something of a good-luck charm for the fans. Football is nothing without the fans and they have this amazing power to make you feel so good or so bad. I loved the Lazio fans and they are highly supportive of their team, but they can be difficult and are a bit of an acquired taste. Sven felt very strongly about the undercurrent of racism in the game and had to make a statement on behalf of the club.

Nothing was really going right – there just seemed to be a build-up of negative energy pushing for change. Our week of holiday could not come soon enough. We decided to spend a few days at Christmas with my parents. I had chosen a wonderful, romantic venue for our New Year's Eve celebrations so that we could forget the world and spend some quality time together: a lovers' hotel, snuggled into a Tuscan village between Florence and Siena, called La Locanda dell'Amorosa.

As the year started Sven was beset with doubts again: perhaps the team was not with him – definitely some players were for him and some against. There are always intricate politics within a team when the position of manager is uncertain. The Chairman was firm in his support and Sven will always be grateful that their friendship stood the test of time.

However, the first match of the year, against Napoli – a team on the edge of relegation – altered everything. The humiliating loss was the final straw for everyone. Later, after we had worked off the adrenalin of the day and were talking into the early hours of the morning, Sven said for the first time that he thought it was all over for him with Lazio and he might have no alternative other than to resign. We were both overwhelmed with sadness. I knew we were very close to the end of this chapter of our lives.

Jerome and I were still busy with the plans for the Fregene beach property, but I felt so emotional that even interior design could not distract me from the stress. I knew that this was not the way that Sven wanted to leave Lazio, but there was no point pretending that it was going to get better. In the end it took him only a couple of days to reach the decision to go – although he continued to agonize to the very end. The Lazio Centennial celebrations were due on 11 January and Sven had a meeting with Cragnotti scheduled for 9 January; he knew he must make up his mind by then. He rose early and took the long drive to Formello. Sometimes when you are waiting, hours can seem like days – time is elastic. It is the same as when you are the winning team in a football match and the last two minutes before the final whistle feel like the longest of your life. I decided to walk in the gardens of the Villa Borghese and asked Jerry to keep me company. It was a beautiful, cold, crisp day and, as I walked in the January sunshine, I was struck by another moment of supreme

Wearing that outfit on my way to Downing Street.

Catching the sun in Polynesia on holiday with Sven.

Left: *On the* Nancy One *trying to rearrange the furniture, and* (below) *in the Greek islands.*

Right: *With Susan Davis and Barbara Dein at the Ryokan near Sapporo during the 2002 World Cup.*

Below: *An evening of entertainment for the players' families at the 2006 World Cup. Left to right: Coleen McLoughlin, me, Cheryl Cole.*

Below: *Back at the team hotel having dinner with Sven the day after the third match of the 2006 World Cup.*

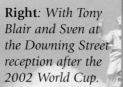

Left: *At the private audience with the Pope organized by Lazio boss Sergio Cragnotti, after Lazio won the Italian league.*

Right: *With Tony Blair and Sven at the Downing Street reception after the 2002 World Cup.*

Below: *With Camilla Parker-Bowles (as she was then) at a private dinner at Highgrove in July 2004 after the announcement of my forthcoming appointment as a Red Cross ambassador.*

Above: *As a presenter at the National Television Awards in 2003.*

A photoshoot after
I was appointed as a
Red Cross ambassador,
taken in 2005.

Below: Talking to
Jack Straw at the
announcement of
Liverpool as the City
of Culture for 2007.

In April 2006, at the annual
Chamber of Commerce awards.
I appeared there as a guest of
honour to introduce the work
of Truce.

Top and top right: *At the 'Balls to War' launch outside the House of Commons, May 2006.*

Above and right: *On my trip to Israel we visited the football pitches built by Truce and watched the children play together, seeing the power of football to bring people together in action.*

Above: *At a special reception at the British Embassy in Israel discussing my work with Truce with Simon McDonald, the Ambassador.*

Right and below: *Meeting Israeli Vice-President Shimon Peres and gaining his support for Truce.*

Above: *In Jerusalem at the Dome of the Rock, feeling inspired by my Jewish ancestors.*

consciousness: my life was going to change and the only way to cope was to trust in destiny. That was the moment Sven made his decision to quit in the car on the way to the meeting.

Sven wanted to do what was best for the club that had given him so much and to which he had brought the greatest success in its hundred-year history. I must admit that I did not want him to resign, because I thought he had more to achieve with the team and I thought he should see out the season. To him, however, results are everything and without the team behind him he believed he could not get the results. He called me at around 1 p.m. to tell me that he had resigned. I started to cry with a mixture of emotions: fear and sadness; joy and expectation; nostalgia for the security of the past and curiosity as a lure cast from the future.

We met for a late lunch and Sven told me that as he was driving he just knew that he could not carry on. He had had an emotional meeting with the players and staff. The Chairman was also visibly upset, but all had agreed it was the best decision for the club. A press conference had been hastily called and Cragnotti congratulated Sven on his term at the club, saying that 'the man who won Lazio the title would always have a second home in Rome.' The negative energy had been transformed.

Lazio's Centennial celebrations were to culminate on 11 January with a match against the Chinese national team and it was decided to combine the event with a farewell tribute to Sven. Looking up, I watched a lunar eclipse above the stadium and thought how it reflected the end of an era. The Chairman gave the Roman imperial salute as a mark of respect and, as Sven stepped forward for a victory circuit, the 35,000-strong crowd exploded with applause. I could see that Sven was overcome with emotion. To be the focus of such an accolade is indescribable.

A few days later Sven made his first trip to London. The decision to quit Lazio early involved settling his contract with England. My domestic life was plunged into a flurry of activity to set up management arrangements for our properties in Italy and to start planning our move to London. Everything was happening so fast there was no real time to adjust. I came to join Sven in London in late January 2001 and we stayed at the Carlton Tower Hotel in Cadogan Square whilst he was setting up his office and organizing his schedule. Sven is incredibly meticulous and, although Tord Grip had been scouting for several months, he was pushing forward with a punishing schedule of match attendance himself. As a result, I was left to my own devices and knew that I would be shuttling backwards and forwards between London and Rome for the next six months.

Meanwhile, the press and photographers were all over us. I remember the first day I arrived at Heathrow. I had not expected to be besieged by photographers as I came out of the VIP section; nor had I expected banner headlines, 'NANCY HAS ARRIVED IN ENGLAND', to be splashed across the papers the following morning. The FA driver who met me at the airport was a real character. He was laughing and trying to explain that there was already massive public curiosity about me. He warned me that the toughest thing would be this press attention. I remember his words to this day, and his gruff Cockney accent: 'The only thing you can believe is true in the papers is the date – and even that you can't be sure of.' But on the whole I was very touched by the warmth of the reception I received, and staying at the Carlton with its close proximity to Chelsea, was a great introduction to the city. Right now, it feels like the capital of the world.

I knew that before we arrived there had been some sabre-rattling from the more conservative elements in English football. Sven had said that, on his first day, arriving at Soho Square, he had been greeted by a corpulent figure dressed in a historic costume (we later found out that this was John Bull – Englishness personified) with a large sign directed at the FA saying 'Hang your heads in shame. We all wanted Terry Venables.' We were both amused by this. The passion for having your say is something we found distinctively English; it is manifest in the great proliferation of publications of all kinds. In fact, we were met with nothing but kindness and consideration everywhere we went. Sven had been given a copy of Niall Edworthy's book *The Second Most Important Job in the Country*, so we knew what to expect and, as the old saying goes, 'If you can't stand the heat, better get out of the kitchen.' We were very green then and didn't know the half of what was yet to come.

My first match and the launch of Sven's career in the United Kingdom was the England friendly at home to Spain at the end of February. Wembley stadium was being rebuilt, so the match was to be held at Villa Park in Birmingham. I went to the match with some of my Italian friends over for the occasion from Rome. It was going to be a very emotional experience seeing Sven play a match as the England manager for the first time. I had had no idea that the etiquette in the Director's box at matches in England was so formal, and on the day I had chosen to wear jeans. No one had told me that this was against the rules. On this occasion the stewards passed my designer jeans, saying, 'It might be a bit harsh to expel the partner of the new England manager at her first game.'

The first thing I noticed was the size of the crowd – the stadium was packed. In Italy it is almost unheard of to have a full house for a friendly. I began to see how football was a kind of religion in this country. The attention Sven received and the public interest in our arrival had opened my eyes to the potential of the positive influence of the game and the great power that football has in the public psyche. The seed of an idea was growing – that I might be able to harness this power for a good cause.

The atmosphere was fantastic on the day as Sven rolled out his new team. Morale in the England camp was high and the players wanted to give their best. Sven was as cool as ever and England passed the first test with flying colours. I knew that

Sven was proud of his choice of players. To face Spain as a first opponent is never an easy task. David Beckham had risen well to the challenge of his first outing as captain.

This was also the first time I met Victoria Beckham – in the last ten minutes when those who need to leave before the crush make their exit. One of the stewards came over to me and said that Victoria was in the corridor outside the director's box and would like to say a quick 'hello' before leaving. I slipped away from my seat and found her waiting with Brooklyn. She was very sweet and charming as she greeted me. 'I just wanted to let you know how happy I am that David was appointed captain,' she said, 'and to wish you both well and say welcome to England.'

As the balance of my time began to be weighted towards London, I began to wind up my affairs in Rome. Despite the lavish suite and great gym, we soon got tired of hotel living and decided to move into a charming little serviced apartment at Hyde Park, directly opposite Kensington Palace. I loved this great green lung in the centre of London and one of my joys was to go for a run early in the morning. I know the Brits complain so much about the weather that it has become a habit, but these days London in the spring can equal Rome or Paris. The apartment would be our base for the next six months whilst I began serious house-hunting. Sven always prefers to live on the outskirts of any big city he is working in; failing that, a park is essential as we are both nature lovers and like to walk.

With the challenge of qualification games facing Sven, I was keen to get all our domestic arrangements in place with as little fuss as possible to give him the maximum support. House-hunting was now a priority and I began to check my hit-list of park-related property postcode by postcode. I loved Hampstead, with its Heath, its old-world high street and Haverstock Hill. Our problem was that it was not central enough. I looked at Belgravia and Chelsea, then fell in love with a beautiful penthouse on Battersea Park overlooking the river – I love to be by the water. But still we hesitated to commit ourselves.

After winning the first three games by the end of April, there was a ten-week break before the next World Cup match, so Sven and I decided to go to Barbados for a little pampering in the sun. We got more Sun than we bargained for. It wasn't the pictures that got to us as much as the taste-less Anglo-Saxon tits-and-bums captions that accompanied them. Neither of us was used to this exploitative invasion of privacy. I had sued photographers for less in Italy – and won – but I decided to let this go and regard it as part of a steep learning curve of managing relationships with the English media. There is always something new to learn in that extraordinary world. Besides, I am not really as litigious as some people think – bikini straps done up or not!

During the spring I started to go to a few matches with Sven and be introduced to the clubs. Slowly I began to meet people and make new friends. Sven was recognized everywhere. But this was a great time for me because I was relatively unknown: I could browse the bookshops or art galleries, find out where to buy things, go to restaurants and just enjoy being in London. After Rome I appreciated the anonymity I had at first in London. I had quite a lot of time on my hands because Sven was going to every match he could – and nobody goes to more matches than Sven. I invited friends from Italy to discover my new city and to show off a little about how quickly I was adapting. My house-hunting continued, but still the feeling of being at home eluded me. We noticed that gardens were a wonderful feature of some of the older London houses and as we both love eating and entertaining al fresco, we now decided a garden would be essential.

After a training session in La Manga in June the England squad was well prepared for their World Cup tie in Athens. All the families of the players and staff were invited and everyone thoroughly enjoyed the opportunity to get to know each other better. The positive results of this for the players were immediately visible when England won their next match against Greece.

Then we found our dream house. I have always loved period architecture and London is a treasure trove of Georgian styles. Actually, our decision to purchase the Nash house at Regent's Park Village was nothing to do with the architecture; the garden is what sold it to us. The terraced lawn slopes gently down to a secluded wild garden banked by mature trees. French windows open on to the sheltered patio in the shade of a well-shaped camellia and magnolia that are a joy in spring. There was ample space on the lawn for t'ai chi and to practise yoga or just relax around the barbecue. No sooner had we bought the house than it was featured in *Hello!*, much to Sven's real anger. Even the mock sycophantic prose style could not carry off the hideous lack of taste. Of course the photographs were nothing to do with us and had been obtained from the estate agent's brochure.

Sven knew if England wanted direct qualification for the World Cup (which they weren't really expecting in 2002), they would have to beat Germany. Defeat in a friendly against Holland brought to an end Sven's run of victories; it was also a timely reminder of the task that lay ahead with Germany. I felt there was a plus in England having a foreign manager when they took on Germany, as he would not be carrying all that history in his backpack. He always thought his England could take on Germany and win.

Sven had a full-strength team and as usual before a match he called me. He was happy and said he was feeling lucky. He really wanted to win the group to show his critics that he was the right man for the job. His dream was to win the World Cup for England just as he had won the Scudetto for Lazio. Sitting on the stands behind him felt just like old times. It was a mild September evening at Munich's Olympic stadium. The atmosphere was so tense you could cut it with a knife. I was sitting in the FA seats with my new friends Barbara Dein and Susan Davies (the wives of Arsenal's David Dein and David

Davies, Executive Director of the FA) and my German friend, Gisella, who is a doctor of alternative medicine. We almost felt as if we were at a home game, as all around were the England fans, with banners held high: 'Eriksson's Army'. Even before the anthems, Gisella said, 'The energies are with England.' I was keen for any positive sign and this was confirmed for me when I saw that the referee was Collina – I always count him as a lucky charm. I looked at Sven and saw him adjust his glasses. I knew he was confident in his team.

England had nothing to lose. There was jubilation in our camp after England had scored three goals, but the Germans struck back and I could see manager Franz Beckenbauer and all the German staff rousing themselves. Gisella, always sensitive to energies, turned to me and said that she felt a change in the atmosphere: she sensed a deflation of energy from the England players. She began to use her arms as antennae as if she was paddling the energies. I couldn't help but laugh at her actions, grateful that she broke my tension over the match at least for a moment. Then, the seemingly impossible happened. Michael Owen scored his third goal. For the first time the England supporters dared think they might win. I could see FA faces looking at the stalwart figure of Sir Geoff Hurst, the famed England striker from the 1966 World Cup win: then I realized that Owen had scored a hat-trick, and against Germany.

But it was not over yet – and Gisella was still cleaning the energies for all she was worth. She had been gathering up the negative wavelengths and then throwing them over her shoulders. Barbara Dein, who was sitting behind, leant over and said that she had a splitting headache. Whether that was from Gisella's energies or the stress of just sitting there we will never know, but the match went on to its unbelievable conclusion: a win for England, five goals to one. I have never been more proud of Sven than at that moment. I could see him as modest and calm as ever at the final whistle. Inside he was on fire with the knowledge of what this would mean to his peers. As he walked to the tunnel I saw Adam Crozier advance to congratulate him. This was more than just a vindication for both of them: it marked the beginning of a new English era.

Sven was not so quick to jump to conclusions. We were only three points behind Germany, but there were still two qualifiers to go with no guarantee. But I know he was very pleased with the whole squad and I think for me this was one of the greatest matches I have ever attended. It was an amazing experience for all and created a new bond between us. For the first time I really felt our adopted country had embraced us at all levels. That night, I heard, there was dancing in Trafalgar Square and, unbelievably, the next day talk of a knighthood for Sven.

Now we had our house I wanted to move our best possessions in and get settled. I can be a home bird as well as a gypsy. The autumn of our first year in England was idyllic, but our peace was shattered by the horror of 9/11 and the devastation of the city of my birth. The horror of the events recurred constantly in my mind.

Back in London, I was still trying to find my feet. Initially, I had spent a fair amount of time by myself, then as we settled into our permanent address I began to receive more and more telephone calls via Sven's assistant at the FA, Tanya. One day the phone rang and a bubbly voice at the other end said, 'Hello Nancy, it's Kay Charlesworth. Do you remember me from Rome? We used to work together at the same law firm.'

Kay had been the English personal assistant to the senior partner at the practice I had been working with when shuttling between New York and Rome. I knew she was passionate about living in Rome and I was surprised to find her back in the UK. 'Kay, I thought you were living in Rome?' I said.

'I was,' she replied, 'but then I moved back and now I am the Bulgari representative in London. We should meet up and I can show you around.' I always love coincidences and it was not long before we met up for dinner and from then on Kay became my new friend and guide to London.

Kay was working on a fascinating Bulgari project which used the storyline of a novel as a medium for product place-ment. This idea was the brainchild of the dashing PR consultant Simon Astaire, who was running the Bulgari account and had commissioned the well-known author Fay Weldon to write the story, which was entitled *The Bulgari Connection*. I thought this was a great project and soon afterwards Kay introduced me to Simon and we all became good friends.

Sven and I were being approached by numerous charities and good causes and we were in danger of being swamped. I wanted to do something new and different in charity work that had not been done before. My passion was helping children in war-torn countries: I know that without peace there is very little chance of reducing poverty or development. Just after 9/11 I felt it was so important to find ways of helping different groups of people understand each other. I had the germ of an idea that the English enthusiasm for football might be mobilized for good causes. I decided to ask Simon if he could help me take this forward.

Simon's PR Company, Protocol, was based at Chelsea Harbour and he had a great young team, mostly working on fashion accounts or representing celebrity clients. He had also worked in the aid-related entertainment world of charity concerts and was well connected in the music industry, counting Sting amongst his closest friends. Above all, he loved football, coming as he did from a family that had always had connections with the sporting world. Later, when we had become friends, Simon mentioned a rather disastrous flirtation that had become very claustrophobic with someone named Ulrika Jonsson.

Simon set up a meeting at the Ritz (another account he was handling) to introduce me to a rather mysterious gentlemen he described as a 'white African chief' who, he said, could help me develop my ideas on football as a charity project. The man he had in mind has since become my very good friend and collaborator, John Carmichael. John was raised in Ghana and had just come from an international peace conference supported by UN Messengers of Peace Luciano Pavarotti and Dame Jane Goodall. They were trying to persuade warring countries in West Africa to declare a day of truce in the hope that a ceasefire might bring about some form of conflict resolution. Unfortunately, the conference had failed. John said that the idea of peace is very abstract and a new big idea was needed with enough incentive to bring parties in conflict to negotiate.

As we tossed ideas around over tea, I became even more convinced that the one force that was strong enough to make the difference was the power of football. All my experience with Sven at Lazio, and now coming to England where passion for the game was so apparent everywhere, made me think that there must be a way to harness that power for good.

We decided that as a next step we would pull together an informal think-tank and give ourselves until the New Year to come up with a plan. My mind went back to my time working in politics and my fascination with Silvio Berlusconi's strategy of building a political power base on football clubs. After the horrific events of 9/11, surely with Sven and England – the home of football – we would be able to persuade the powers behind the game to set aside rival interests for a good cause.

My plan was to talk with Sven about my new idea when the time was right.

For the match against Greece Old Trafford had hung the flags out and there was almost a festival atmosphere. The national anthem was the loudest I have ever heard it sung. It was a difficult match, but England secured a draw and with it qualification for the 2002 World Cup. Sven was very proud and told me later that in the press room the journalists stood up and gave a standing ovation to David Beckham for his last-minute goal. This was unheard of.

If ever there was a honeymoon time for us in England, this was it. Sven was almost universally respected. Having brought on the golden generation of English football, he had transformed the prospects of the national team. As his partner I was treated like royalty and there was goodwill and kindness wherever we went. As we approached the end of our first year, I could not have been happier. But my thoughts began to turn to my own career and the possibility of using my new-found situation for some positive good. I felt a real desire to give something back for all my good fortune.

After the year-long roller-coaster ride on the road to qualification we were both in need of some serious rest and relaxation. Sven had recently been voted the UK Coach of the Year and the award ceremony had been scheduled for 16 December with the presentation by Princess Anne. He was very proud, as a foreign manager, to receive this national accolade. This was our first Christmas in England, but after the

Boxing Day football matches (a tradition found only in England) we would leave to seek sun, sea and sand for the New Year. This time we chose Mauritius as our destination haven. We could not wait to get away.

However, I knew that Sven would have to conclude the World Cup draw formalities in Busan, South Korea first. I was glad to stay in London as Sven flew halfway across the world for the draw. Unfortunately England drew a very difficult group. When Sven returned we both knew that the New Year would bring some serious challenges. We were eager to take time out just to re-orientate and ground ourselves without disturbance. I thought this would be a good time to break the news of my plans for my new project.

TRUCE

●

If we could all read the secret history of our enemies;
we should find in each man's life sorrow and
suffering enough to disarm all hostilities.

HENRY WADSWOTH LONGFELLOW

MAURITIUS WAS BLISS. IT WAS MARK TWAIN WHO suggested that Mauritius was made first and that heaven is only a poor copy of it. I would have to agree. But, in football, holidays are all too brief. Sven's next commitment was the draw for the European Championships in Portugal in 2004. Happy to be back in our own home in London, I could set about preparing to launch my new project. I had spoken to Sven about the ideas I had discussed with Simon Astaire and Johnny Carmichael, and he was intrigued to know more.

I was looking forward to John's return from Ghana, where he had been taking Christmas and the New Year to review the Meridian link scheme between Ghana and Greenwich. The programme, based on a Millennium civic twinning, was designed to link countries and cities on the Greenwich Meridian and was called 'Zero Degrees of Separation'. Our aim was to play football 'down the line', but we needed an overarching concept to bring it all together. We all hoped to convene our think-tank in January. The plan was to launch the idea with an event in early May in tandem with the England squad announcement. Bearing Sven's position in mind, we knew that we would have to do everything by the book and consult with the football family to avoid falling foul of the convoluted politics of English football.

The draw in Portugal for the European Championships promised an easier ride for England, but then the newspapers began to run a campaign against Sven, questioning his loyalty to the England team. We decided to take a break at a secret hideaway in the Algarve where we knew no one could find us. First there were claims in the press that Sven's old club, Lazio, wanted him back and then, when Sir Alex Ferguson announced his retirement, the press found an opportunity to rack up the tempo on Sven's doing a deal. Of course there are professional ethics, contractual obligations and loyalty to employers, but in Europe looking at alternative opportunities is neither precluded nor treated as a crime. People consider their professional options all the time, but that does not mean that they will be taken up; you can look but not touch. Sven's loyalty was always to England and his players. His greatest ambition was the World Cup and he always believed that England gave him the greatest opportunity to achieve that. I certainly knew nothing about any contact, and Sven and I did not discuss it.

The story of the famous First World War Christmas truce, when the German and British soldiers played football in the trenches, had been featured in the media over the Christmas period. This piece of history is not as well known in Europe as it is in Britain and I had not heard about this extraordinary event before. I was amazed to think that ordinary soldiers from both sides were able to rediscover their common humanity by the simple, spontaneous act of playing football together. At our brainstorming sessions at Chelsea Harbour, the truce story began to form the focal point of our plans for an international kickabout – Kick a Ball for Peace. Having worked with the United Nations Peace Messengers on conflict resolution, John explained some of the background to the UN International Day of Peace, originally proposed by the British government, to be held on 21 September each year, and Simon wanted to build pitches. If I pulled it all together using the Christmas truce as an example, we had our project. Then Susie Smith, acting co-ordinator for our initiative, said, 'Why don't we call the project Truce?'

I was first introduced to the Labour MP Ann Taylor (now Baroness Taylor) by David Davies during one of the World Cup qualifying games in 2001. I was drawn to her immediately, perhaps through our shared passion for both politics and football. Ann was about to go on holiday to Rome with her young daughter and asked me for some advice about what to see and do. I offered to help find tickets for a Serie A football match – I think it was the Roma versus Juventus game that we selected. At that time Ann was on the board of the Football Foundation and understood very well the sensitivities and complexities of the English football family. She offered to help our fledgling organization find its feet and introduced us to the parliamentary football team (Parliament FC), who went on to become ambassadors for football for peace. John and I had thought about visiting New York to consult the UN Secretary General, Kofi Annan, to discuss a football component to the UN Day of Peace. When I mentioned this to Ann in the new year, she offered to connect us to the UK's mission to the UN.

With the momentum behind the Truce project growing, I decided that it was time to involve Sven. Lunch was booked at The Ritz, and Sven and I met with John and Simon to discuss strategy. For Sven to become patron we would need the approval of the FA: the England manager was supposed to be winning the World Cup, not being distracted by charity functions. Sven suggested a meeting with Adam Crozier to present the project and seek his advice. After seeking endorsement from the UN, we then planned to go to Zurich to gain the support of Sepp Blatter, President of FIFA, football's governing body. If we had backing from those two, the rest should be fairly straightforward. We should have known better. In the world of football politics, nothing is straightforward. But at least we had a plan.

A friendly game against Holland had yielded a respectable draw for England but Sven's positioning of players attracted press criticism. He likes to keep his options open and the fact that he had not made up his mind on the squad until the last minute was always going to be an issue with the press. Sven doesn't care about these things. His priority is football, but sometimes you have to include the press in your thought process if you want them to understand your decisions. I think, in a way, although he knew it was an important part of his job, sometimes Sven would have liked to avoid the media, as so often involvement led to huge complications and distraction from the job in hand. Finding a balance was not easy but, to be fair to all, it was the only way. I would never interfere with Sven's relationship with the press over his job – in fact, I think he handled it really well. However, in other matters with the press Sven and I often disagreed over the way to handle things. Sven is genuinely shy and I think this often led the press to jump to conclusions about his being aloof or having a deliberate policy to exclude. Sven may be detached, but he is not aloof. His players know that well.

Although I still did some consulting, during our relationship Sven had never known me to have a project that consumed the majority of my time. Due to the demands of his career I had always had to be the flexible one – a choice that seemed natural and one I was very happy with at the time, as our relationship could not have flourished without it. I had always been there for him as a partner without distraction, and perhaps he was a bit spoiled. Now, with my growing commitments to Truce, a hectic social schedule and the complexities of his football diary, we began to find that our time together was being squeezed out. I was spending more time in the company of the young and vibrant group of people who were taking Truce forward and, perhaps, Sven began to feel that I was not always there for him. I can't say that he did not want me to do the Truce project, as he was always supportive. However, I think we had not realized the full implications of the demands on my time or the energy that I would throw into it. I don't just like to cut the ribbon at the fête; I like to get my hands dirty – and the prospect of going to Israel or Africa to build football pitches or help war-affected children excited me. After a while, perhaps Sven began to resent this intrusion into our time together.

I was looking forward to my visit to New York to talk with the UN, but I had a real sense of foreboding as well. The world had changed in the aftermath of 9/11 and I knew that I would find it unsettling – like visiting a parallel universe. John and I were guests of Sir Jeremy Greenstock, UK Representative to the UN and a very experienced diplomat. Sir Jeremy had been a housemaster at Eton, so he knew all about young people and the story of the Christmas truce. We found his advice in navigating the complex world of the UN invaluable. He would later go to Iraq as UK Representative and was present when Truce worked in partnership with Team Iraq to facilitate the visit to England of the Iraqi national football team on their Football for Peace tour in 2004.

Arriving in New York was quite different on this occasion

and, although New Yorkers were their usual indomitable selves, there was a feeling of disbelief over what had happened, as though the city was still stunned. When we visited Ground Zero to pay our respects we found the eerie sense of tragedy experienced on battlefields or in places where great suffering has occurred. There were many visitors and the boards were hung with cards and keepsakes from the tens of thousands who had come. In a way, I will be sad when they rebuild this site, covering over the open space that has let the green heart of Manhattan breathe again. Afterwards, I felt compelled to go with John to the Roman Catholic Cathedral of St Patrick on 5th Avenue to rest in the atmosphere of that sacred space and heal my soul. As we headed for the briefing meeting with Sir Jeremy, the impact of the visit to Ground Zero made us feel that the world was in desperate need of a big project for peace in which people everywhere could participate.

Kofi Annan was on an overseas visit, so we met with Deputy Secretary General Madame Louise Fréchette, who received us with great warmth. She expressed the UN's wish to promote international projects for peace-building and conflict resolution throughout the world and endorsed the idea that the proposed UN Day of Peace would provide an ideal opportunity for us simultaneously to hold a day of Football for Peace. Madame Fréchette welcomed the new England manager's support for the project and agreed to set up a UN connection to work with us. We were introduced to Patrick Hayford, a larger-than-life Ghanaian, who had been

High Commissioner for Ghana in London and whom John had met several times before. Patrick was now Director for African Affairs for the United Nations, reporting directly to Kofi Annan. He told us that the Secretary General was an ardent football fan and – after the Ghanaian Black Stars, of course – would love to see Sven's England win the World Cup. Everybody was in full agreement that football was one of the few human activities that had universal acceptance and for which everybody knew the rules. If there was any force on earth that could *stop* the world for a day – to mark a global ceasefire – then it would be football. We spoke about the World Cup and the fact that, when the big matches are being played, combatants put down their guns and turn on their television sets – a phenomenon well known to the UN Blue Berets in conflict zones.

John and I left feeling that we had the makings of an international campaign. I could not wait to get back to Sven to tell him that Kofi Annan was keeping a watchful eye on England.

Unfortunately, when I returned I found some of the press were agitating over Sven's management style. Things got a bit fractious when I was trying to tell him about my trip to New York and he was thinking of player permutations for the next friendly against Italy – I think you might say that we were getting on each other's nerves. We have always had what others might describe as a turbulent relationship, although absolutely solid at its core. We are both strong personalities; when we fight the sparks can fly. I have to admit I am not the easiest person to live with and I do have a quick temper. Sven goes cold and broody whilst I like to get everything out in the open. We are both a bit of a handful at times. But although we certainly appear to react very differently to difficult circumstances, at the core Sven and I react the same way to so many things. Sometimes it's easy to get distracted by my keenness to confront and Sven's keenness to avoid issues, but it is so important to understand the common ground that underlies this. So often, people are too distracted by surface differences to see the common bond that is ultimately stronger than anything else.

After New York, in preparation for our meeting with Adam Crozier, John and I obtained a copy of his policy document for the FA giving his vision and purpose for the organization: 'To use the power of football to build a better future.' This exactly reflected the ethos of the Truce campaign and our plan, devised with the backing of the UN, to launch a national day of Football for Peace in the UK as a pilot project for the world event. Even in New York, staff at the UN were aware of the success of large charity fundraising projects in Britain, like Children In Need or Comic Relief's Red Nose Day. The British people are very generous in their giving and the country can boast one of the most effective voluntary sectors in the world. If the UN Day of Peace could be supported by a national day of Football for Peace, then it could spread throughout the rest of the world. I believed that, in this way, the UN day might grow teeth and become an effective day of global truce.

Although I had met Adam before, I had never encountered him in a work-related situation. He was as charming as ever, and gave close and detailed consideration to our proposals. When we had finished, he mentioned the cause-related marketing department he had started up at Saatchi & Saatchi – he thought this initiative would have been just their sort of project. In principle, he thought ours was a great idea but he had one problem, and that was starting a charity around the England coach. He explained that there are so many examples of celebrity charities running into trouble and causing grief for all involved; he could not afford to have this happen to the England manager. However, he suggested that if we were looking at organizing a campaign that included existing charities and that could cooperate with the FA International Department, then we may all be on to something great. He suggested a meeting with David Davies and Jane Bateman at the FA International to explore ways of working together.

In the meantime, the next friendly against Italy was approaching. Even though I always enjoy watching England and Italy, on the day it was disappointing. I have never really been able to get excited over friendly matches because you know that the players sometimes feel they have to hold themselves back in order to avoid injury. At the very last moment, Italy scored to win the game. We both knew the press would have a field day. Of course, Sven had his reasons for his tactics, but this bears no weight with press opinion. He likes to let the waves wash over him and to ignore the bad news. I think we

both recognized that this was a difficult time in our relationship; we were both a little distant and preoccupied. But I
never expected Sven to allow himself the loss of judgement
that would turn our lives upside down.

On the day that Sven was due to announce the squad for the
match against Paraguay, we woke up to find the press
encamped outside our front door. Although by now I was
getting used to the newspapers' interest in Sven's life, the
sheer number of them on this occasion was very unusual. I
had woken earlier than normal and while I was in the bathroom I noticed there was a lot of noise outside – usually our
street is so quiet. I opened the blind to see what was going on
and below me the street was teeming with reporters. Since
then it's become almost a compulsion for me to check the
street through the bathroom blind every morning. I like to be
prepared. I asked Sven if he knew what was going on and,
looking very preoccupied, he said that he had no idea. Then,
as Sven was leaving to go to the office, I took a call from an
Italian journalist friend of mine who told me that a story had
broken of Sven and another woman. Of course, I didn't even
consider it, but I called after Sven to ask him if he knew
anything about this. He said he didn't, but that he would try
to find out more and would call me from the office as soon as
he could. He seemed a little concerned, but I didn't let it
worry me.

I was due to attend a Truce meeting at the Carlton Towers
Hotel that morning with Simon Astaire and Johnny

Carmichael, before going on to a meeting at the Afghan Embassy. When I arrived, Simon – who was also my agent at the time – was on the phone and had a copy of the *Daily Mirror* in his hand. He looked very concerned. When he finished the call, he held the newspaper up in front of me and I was shocked to see the headline: 'SVEN AND ULRIKA'S SECRET AFFAIR'. My blood ran cold; I could not believe it. First the call from my Italian friend and now this story in the newspaper. I vaguely remembered meeting Ulrika Jonsson very briefly at a party held by Richard Desmond, but I couldn't understand how she could possibly be connected to Sven. Nobody said anything.

My first reaction was to confront the allegation head on. 'This is rubbish,' I said. 'Maybe we should sue the *Mirror* and I will get them to give the money to Truce.'

I needed to be alone, so I walked away to try to speak to Sven. He was in a meeting but I left a message. Surely he must have seen the paper himself; someone would have shown him. I knew he couldn't leave his meeting, but I was so frustrated at having to wait. I paced up and down looking at my phone as I waited for him to return my call.

As soon as he was free Sven phoned me back. His voice was quiet and husky with embarrassment when he spoke. This was unlike him and I hardly knew where to begin. My first question was to ask if he had seen the headline, and then to ask him if it was true.

We decided that we couldn't possibly talk freely on the

phone. He tried to reassure me, telling me not to worry and that he would explain everything when we were together at home that afternoon. I may be naive, but when the man you love and trust tells you that something like this is not true, you have to believe him. I grasped at that straw, knowing I had to return to my meeting and maintain my composure. However, I was angry and wanted to blame someone for what I thought was a smear campaign against Sven. I turned on Simon, asking him, 'What do you know about this?' He said that he knew nothing.

Johnny asked whether I had any news from Sven. My head was spinning and I could hardly think. 'He said it was rubbish and not to worry. We're going to speak later,' I heard myself say.

I was feeling so confused and miserable. There had been something in Sven's voice, and, however much I denied it, deep down I was beginning to have some doubts. I knew I had to get out of the Carlton Towers. Gathering my bag and coat I started to leave in search of fresh air. Johnny asked me if I needed some company and Simon said he would make some enquiries to try to find out what was behind it all. I needed to find a refuge and somewhere to think.

The press reported that I went out on a shopping spree that day. In fact, Johnny and I went from the Carlton Towers to the Brompton Oratory, the church I had always turned to since my arrival in England. I always feel drawn to sacred places in times of need, whether they be church, synagogue or mosque. The spiritual energy is protective and feels like a blanket around your soul. I needed some time to collect my thoughts – as I say, 'to make a telephone call to myself' – so I walked around on my own for half an hour to reflect on my life and try to banish the fears, doubts and insecurities that assailed me. My temper was rising, but I didn't know who to get angry with.

As I walked quietly around the church, my mind was in turmoil. I didn't know who or what to believe. I could not believe the story was true. Surely Sven, in his position, could not be so foolish? I loved him and I knew, whatever people were saying, that he loved me; I have never doubted that. After all we had been through together, his patience in waiting for me whilst I made up my mind to leave my ex-husband and his courage in telling Giancarlo of our affair, I never for one moment thought he would jeopardize our relationship. I was absolutely sure that the story must be untrue; the newspaper must have got it wrong. But I still had this sinking feeling in my stomach.

As I stepped out on to the street, there was a mild drizzle in the air. Johnny asked if I was all right and I assured him that I was, so we said our goodbyes. My therapy on that day was first to pray and then to carry on determinedly as normal. I did some food shopping, then decided to head home to start preparing dinner.

My driver, Terry, who has been like a rock to me throughout our trials and tribulations, picked me up to take me home. As we drove along, I looked out through the rain at the grey streets of London and they did not seem as friendly as they had just yesterday. Suddenly I was freezing, a shiver running down my spine, and I had to ask Terry to turn down the air-conditioning.

When I got home, Sven was already there. He, too, was sheltering from the media storm. The press were still filling the street outside the house and it had been almost impossible to get the car through the gate. They were all furiously taking pictures as I took the two steps from the car to the front door. I realized that Sven had already run this gauntlet. Although one or two photographers had sometimes followed us around in England, this level of attention was unbelievable. It seemed ridiculous to me that anything short of a huge international incident should have drawn this much attention.

Throughout that afternoon and evening, Sven told me in his own words something of the very brief and meaningless affair. He was full of apologies and some bittersweet denials. I simply wanted all this attention to go away and our lives to get back to normal, even though I knew it would take time to straighten it out in my own mind.

On Saturday, I just hibernated for the day. I knew that Sven had a meeting with Adam Crozier to discuss the implications of the press story for his job and I knew he was not going to comment about his private life. Afterwards, he was going to the Chelsea match. In the evening, we had intended to go to San Lorenzo – our favourite restaurant – and did not want to feel forced into changing our plans. I also spoke to Simon that afternoon, who told me that Ulrika's agent had been stoking the fire with the press, as Ulrika had a book coming out shortly. I resolved to mention this to Sven when he returned.

In the late afternoon, when he arrived home after the game, Sven seemed flustered and agitated. I knew that all the attention and speculation was getting to him and that the last couple of days in the spotlight had been hell for a man who is essentially shy and intensely private. I knew he probably didn't want to talk about it, but I was worried by what Simon had told me about the possibility of this being some kind of publicity stunt. Sven said he was annoyed because Ulrika had also been at the Chelsea match that afternoon, and that the press had had a field day.

I was angry, but I decided to concentrate on our present, not on what had already happened and could not be changed. For now, the press situation was growing more serious by the moment. It is very difficult living your relationship in front of the media and, although in many ways I would much rather have stayed at home that evening, I didn't want to allow the press to have such control over our lives. I mustered all my courage, threw back my hair and headed for Beauchamp Place with my man. Again, it was practically impossible for Sven to get the car out of the drive, the press pack was crowding the gate so closely. I forced myself to ignore their shouts and the flashing of cameras right in our faces. As always, I had taken time over my appearance – not for the gratification of the paparazzi outside, but because I needed to feel that I was valuing myself. It gave me at least a semblance of normality and the confidence to distance myself from the mob outside. On my finger, I wore my diamond ring. The next day, that diamond ring featured in all the reports as though it was a new present from Sven. In fact, it was the engagement ring that Sven gave me on our first Christmas together. I am wearing it still. In fact, I had been photographed many times in the intervening years wearing the ring and I was amazed that the press would make up such a story when that same ring had featured in so many pictures since 1999.

On the Sunday morning we were woken by the telephone at about 8.30 a.m. Sven got up and took the call in his office. I began to doze off again. When he returned about ten minutes later he sat down on the bed and spoke my name in a voice that I will never forget. I opened my eyes. He looked very sheepish. 'Nancy,' he said. 'There is more rubbish in the papers today that will make you unhappy.'

I said nothing, but my stomach tightened into a knot and my skin went very cold. I think, deep down in the back of my mind, my subconscious had known all along that things were not right in our relationship, but my conscious self had not accepted it.

Like all men in their weakness, Sven looked like a little boy forlorn. The story was splashed all over the tabloids. He told me that he had felt publicly humiliated when Ulrika had turned up at the match the day before. I knew that she could never have had any genuine feelings for him or she would never have paraded herself in such a way. We realized that he had been set up, that it had all been about money and publicity, and that he had been completely foolish.

Although we decided to get on with our lives and ignore the press, they would not ignore us. In spite of their presence, we began to work things out. As everyone knows, there are many people who, thinking they are being clever, live by the motto that if they are caught, they should just lie and deny. Believe me, this is a bad idea. The truth and a good clean confession will always be the best way and, if there is still love, it will conquer anything. There was still a real strength to be found in our love and we held on tight to it. But forgiveness does not come easy and working through the consequences of such betrayal will always take time.

Looking back, I know I should have seen the signs, but I trusted Sven and thought he had more sense. I don't know what details the newspapers reported. I don't know any other details either, because I didn't ask. That isn't my story, it's Sven's and he can tell it if he wants to. You make a choice, and I chose not to read those stories and not to listen to what people were saying, even my friends. If it's your life and your relationship, you've got to take responsibility for it; no one else can really know what you should do. Perhaps it was just coincidence that Ulrika's book was due to come out after the World Cup. Sven said that he had no rational explanation for how he could have made such a big mistake. He felt that he had been used and begged me to forgive him.

An old proverb says that true love is like a sword and has to go through fire and water to be tempered. I felt that the sword of our love had been honed enough for both of us. Sven suffered huge damage to his own self-respect. He knew that he had tarnished his image and that he would never have quite the same admiration from the English again. By falling below his own standards, he had lost his sense of self-esteem and that good old Nordic guilt wouldn't leave him alone. But the Sven and Nancy story was a romance long before we came to England and our love could not so easily be broken. I was a bit bemused to hear that newspaper columnists were commenting on the future of our relationship – it seemed so bizarre that they should be wasting their energy on it. The plain truth is that human relationships are extremely complex and you can't judge others unless you are on the inside. The only thing that can keep people together is their choice to love each other and their courage to carry on doing so even when they fall short of their self-imposed ideals.

That Sunday, we spent the day quietly at home, each trying to work through our pain – in Sven's case guilt, and in mine hurt. In the afternoon the lovely weather drew us outside and we decided to have our tea in the garden. Sven broke the silence: 'It is incredible how we have to come so close to losing something before we know how important it is.'

I was aware that, with both of us being so busy over the last six months, we had lost some of the intimacy of our relationship. I asked him if there was something I had done or not done that had provoked this. I could see that I had touched some nerve or sensitive point. I could sense a trace of his wounded pride, as if by being with others or doing something for myself I was in some way neglecting him. Suddenly, I became suspicious of the cultural chauvinism of the football world. Had their Chinese whispers stoked the fires of the negative publicity against Sven? Although I had no real reason to suspect them, I began to speculate whether the awkwardness of Sven's relationship with certain factions of the football fraternity might have led to some part of our problems with the press.

That night we had a kitchen supper *à deux*, still nursing the wounds inflicted on each other. We were, and are, really a wedded couple without the paperwork and are used to talking about our relationship and its ups and downs. Our love was born in a desperate trial of relationships and we could ride this new trial out, too, if we stuck together and rediscovered our trust. In a perverse way, perhaps Sven had to test my love for him and the affair was just a ploy to attract my attention. That is why, in our relationship, the issues are always about us and not about any other.

I knew Monday was going to be a nightmare of a day as the story was going to be everywhere, including Sweden and Italy, with all the embarrassment that that would entail for our families. Sven also had a press conference arranged to launch the new England World Cup suit in the afternoon and that was going to be like stepping into the lion's den.

Sven was full of self-recrimination that his weakness had left him open to being used. I knew then that all contact with Ulrika was all over and that whatever came from the other side it would be frozen out. Sven wanted his life back. How the world can change in a week. I decided to maintain a dignified silence, as there was nothing to talk about. I was not going to engage in a war of words over what amounted to a common male peccadillo. Of course I was hurt, but the most important thing was that we loved each other and after such a trial love can grow stronger.

On the Wednesday we decided to drive out of London to have lunch at one of our favourite places, the Waterside Inn at Bray, on the way to Oxford. This little break from our usual routine gave us a chance to talk and to try to rekindle our relationship. After this trauma, our love affair was as passionate as ever. You have to work at waking up your love for each other to maintain its intensity. Sadly, this often only happens at times of great loss or suffering and when, like the song, 'you don't know what you've got till it's gone.'

The week I made the front page in England was not the way I had imagined it would be. Becoming a household name overnight is a bit of a shock to the system. A few insiders knew who I was before, but people on the street would pass by without a second glance. After this week all of that changed. My one enduring memory of this time of great joy and sadness was the support and warmth of the British people, as expressed by the fans and players at a packed Highbury stadium when Arsenal played West Ham. Sven and I arrived together late and the players were already on the pitch. I was wearing a white suit and stood out from the crowd a little as I walked to find my seat. Suddenly, I could hear the sound of applause led by the players on the pitch. At first I did not know what was going on, then I heard my name: 'Nancy, Nancy.' It was an unforgettable experience as the crowd picked up the chant and some threw flowers. Tears came to my eyes and I had that strange feeling of ascension, when you find yourself the centre of attention of a live crowd of many thousands. I felt so honoured by this spontaneous outpouring of sympathy from so many. Even when I sat down the applause did not stop. I have never in my life known anything like that – it was one of the most uplifting moments I am ever likely to experience. I could see that Sven was shocked by the attention. It was clear that the fans wanted an end to the scandal and to salvage their dreams of World Cup glory.

During that whole time, Sven's only comment to reporters was 'What is private has to stay private,' but it was already public in a way that neither of us could ever have expected. I tried to bear myself with dignity under a spotlight that I had not sought at a time when I was at my most vulnerable. I shall always be grateful to the British people – and Arsenal, my team – for the privilege of this once-in-a-lifetime experience. People do need people, and the public sympathy helped to heal the public exposure. This experience truly confirmed my belief that one should never take people for granted and should always show sympathy and respect for anyone in pain.

Forgiveness is a gift. It is like a human form of grace and you can't just turn it on. It is an emotion born out of loving someone beyond a hurt to oneself.

After the scandal and my forgiveness, Sven was greatly relieved to get back to what he really loves doing more than anything else – football. The World Cup was less than two months away. During this time we were both preoccupied with our respective work, although we were now very careful not to neglect our relationship. I picked up the Truce baton as we prepared to launch the campaign on the day the England squad would be announced at a Truce lunch in aid of the Variety Club of Great Britain.

Before this interruption to our lives, Ann Taylor, knowing of my background in Italian politics, had rung to ask if I would like to have lunch at the House of Commons and experience the British way of doing things. We had a wonderful lunch and then, as it was a Wednesday, Ann asked if I would like to attend Prime Minister's Question Time as a guest in the public gallery. This was a great surprise and I jumped at the chance, since I had only seen it on TV. Watching live was tremendous and very much like attending a performance. The atmosphere was a little like the Roman senate, but with all the quaint charm of the gallery.

But Ann's afternoon of surprises was not over. She had

something even more amazing planned, as she turned to me and asked in a casual way, 'Would you like to meet the Prime Minister?' I was taken aback, as in Italy it is not so easy to meet the First Minister informally – but I didn't hesitate and said that there was nothing I would like better. We met in Tony Blair's private office at the House of Commons directly after Question Time for about fifteen minutes. It was all so natural and spontaneous, and I was flattered by his sense of humour and charm. He had met Sven before and told me he was a Newcastle fan. Naturally, I was able to plug my Truce campaign and he offered his support to make it all happen.

I was delighted. Now Truce had the support of the United Nations, the FA and the British Prime Minister. All we needed was a successful launch event to give wings to my dream and issue the challenge. I knew that we were too late to lock down an event for the 2002 World Cup in Japan, but we could plan for a future event and start the good work by delivering football facilities to war children around the world. With the help of the parliamentary football team, we hoped to assist with the reconstruction of the Afghan national stadium in Kabul and open a dialogue with the Peres Centre for Peace in Israel to help facilitate football exchanges between Palestinian and Israeli youth. But first we would start at home to help the Variety Club, with the possibility of intervening in the growth of gang conflict on the streets of London. The war zones were not only in far-away developing countries – they were in our own back yard.

Following my meeting with Adam Crozier, John and I had met with David Davies and his international team at the FA, led by Jane Batemen and Kim Fisher. The FA had lost the last bid to host the World Cup in England and one reason cited was its lack of international engagement. Therefore, the FA had established a department which had already done some fantastic work with minimal resources, and had put together a portfolio of football-related projects in affiliated countries around the world – a great contribution to international football development. It was only natural for us to want to build on their foundation and expand their work into a nationwide project. Sadly, after Adam Crozier's departure from the FA, this department was set aside and one of the most innovative projects that the FA had started was never fully realized.

One of the projects initiated was at the outbreak of the war in Afghanistan, when a team from the international peace-keeping force and the local Afghan FA set up a series of friendly matches for fostering better community relations. Alastair Campbell had been involved in liaising between Downing Street and the FA. The hope was that Sven and I might go down to 'kick off' a match in Kabul. As it was, the situation proved too dangerous and, although the football matches went ahead, it was felt better not to put the England manager in harm's way. I heard later that an Afghan minister had been killed at the airport at the time we were due to be there, so no doubt it was the right decision.

The Truce launch was scheduled for Thursday, 9 May 2002, as a lunch ahead of the squad announcement. This would follow a tightly run schedule, as Sven had to be bang on time for the FA conference after lunch. The whole event had to be carefully synchronized and coordinated with the FA, as millions would be sitting on the edge of their seats waiting to know who had been picked to represent their country. We were also hosting, as our guests of honour, the Afghan FA and the Afghan Olympic Association. The Variety Club was the chosen charity and Jarvis Astaire – Simon's uncle – had been instrumental in liaising between the organizations. The Truce exhibition, illustrating Football for Peace and sport therapy in conflict zones, was organized by Susie Smith and our team of young volunteers.

With so many injury scares among the England players, Sven had been hedging his bets and, having postponed the announcement once, he knew that he had to make a final decision. Our prize of the day was the twenty-three names of the squad – only to be revealed after the public announcement had been made – written by Sven on his event menu. I saw a number of gentlemen trying to peer over his shoulder as he was writing. The lunch raised £35,000 for the Variety Club and, as Sven departed, guests and the nation waited for the announcement.

After all the build-up, we had a huge sense of anticipation as we approached the World Cup. I had put the last few traumatic weeks behind me and was really looking forward to my first World Cup on the inside. This was Sven's dream and mine: that England and the new golden generation of football talent would win. A six-day rest and recuperation lay-over to acclimatize the squad had been planned in Dubai. Ahead of that, David and Victoria Beckham had planned a send-off party at their beautiful home in Hertfordshire. Family and close friends, along with the good and the great from show-business and football, had been invited for a garden party to get us all into a winning mindset. The guests were an eclectic élite and I always enjoy watching the way in which people from different walks of life present themselves. You could see Sir Richard Branson rubbing shoulders with Mohamed Al Fayed. Cilla Black was there, and Jamie Oliver. Apart from the current England players, there was Sir Geoff Hurst, and other knights, including Sir David Frost and Sir Elton John. Once again I was reminded of the story of the Arthurian Round Table, with the World Cup as the Grail and, instead of twelve knights, our band of brothers of eleven players. It was a great party for me. I wore a fabulous turquoise beaded gown – one of my favourites – designed by Randolph Duke of my home town, New York, and, apart from that, nothing – except diamonds. It was all a beautiful game and, as I walked in, a journalist asked me if the gown and the diamonds were presents from Sven. 'Most definitely,' I laughed, treating this deep and incisive question with the gravitas it deserved. 'Sven loves to give me presents.'

There were no illusions about the task ahead and the challenge. The gladiators knew they were in what was known as the Group of Death, but they had qualified against the odds and beaten Germany. The players felt confident in their manager and the manager was proud of his team. The country expected the best from them.

Arriving at the Jumeirah Beach Club in Dubai was the first time I realized the scale of the England operation. The players, their families and staff were over a hundred-strong and made up an entire holiday village. For me this was a time to chill and enjoy the beach. Sven was always on edge as he dealt with injury issues, which needed constant monitoring and management in order to field an optimum side. I was looking forward to Japan, as I love oriental culture, and had a feeling that this would be a unique World Cup. I felt sure that the location might stop some of the more chauvinistic elements of football emerging and prevent some of the more violent pursuits of the European game. When the team left for Japan, I flew back with the rest of the wives and girlfriends to London for a few days. My plan was to link up with Barbara Dein and Susan Davies and for the three Ds – Dell'Olio, Dein and Davies – to warm up in Rome as a stopover on our way to Japan and all the excitement.

When the team arrived in Osaka on 25 May, it was to a festival atmosphere. England had been adopted by the Japanese as their twin team and the players had all been made honorary Japanese 'citizens'. I think Beckhamania can take credit for this. Sven told me that they were almost stampeded to death as David was mobbed by female fans in their quest to touch him. The three Ds arrived in Japan to be given a trip around Tokyo Bay and a sightseeing tour of the capital. We loved the bright lights of the big city, the wonderful food, the beautiful people and the discovery of karaoke. And, throughout, we three women were constantly escorted by the gallant gentlemen of the press. We had a ball.

By tradition, World Cup group games are always a bit tense and erratic. The first test would be Sweden, always a difficult side for England. I think the England team felt all the more confident for having Sven on their side, for who better to catch the Swedes than a Swede? The stadium was packed with English supporters, plus a big Japanese audience who had come to see their favourite international team. The match ended in a draw. England hadn't lost, but morale had suffered a big blow, and Sven said afterwards that the atmosphere in the dressing room had been like a funeral. It had always been my habit to go down to see Sven after matches outside the dressing room before he went to give his press conferences. It was a moment for swift congratulations or just a kiss before the public reclaimed him – it was always a few hours before I saw him again. It was no different at the World Cup. The Japanese officials might have been surprised, but I was always escorted by someone from the FA through security to outside the dressing room after every match when it was possible. I've been told that I'm the only woman to have got so close to the dressing rooms at such a time.

Sven knew he had to lift the team's spirits, so he organized a free day to get out and about or just relax. Up in the mountains, Susan, Barbara and I stayed in a traditional Japanese inn, a *riyokan*. We delighted in sleeping on the floor, dressing in kimonos and watching a special show of traditional arts and dancing. Afterwards, in the bar, having a final drink before bed, we were comically dismayed to find a striptease beginning. At the same time I noticed that the bar was full of English press who were taking photos of us and the strippers. Of course, we left immediately, reporting the lapse of security to the FA as we were so worried that it would be spun badly in the papers. Fortunately it was never reported so, looking back, the three of us can tell our ridiculous story happily.

England's big test lay ahead. Argentina were joint favourite with France to win the World Cup, and England knew this team was a serious obstacle in the path of their progress. Sven believed if the team could win this match, they could go all the way. And he was sure they could. Sven felt Argentina was a team of very talented and skilful individuals, but if England was the better team on the day, they could win. It was his job to make sure they were the better team. Despite all the press doom and gloom after the disappointing performance against Sweden, Sven was not at all dismayed and just got on with the job of preparation. The stadium at Sapporo was filled with supporters from both sides. There was a lot at stake for Argentina, too. After defeat in the Falklands War and severe economic recession at home, they had much to prove. Sven told me this was always going to be a matter of national pride.

I was delighted to learn that the referee for the match would be Pierluigi Collina; at least we knew the decisions would be impartial. The teams were pretty evenly matched at the start, and I was so happy that the players seemed to have shaken off the nerves they displayed against Sweden. In the end, David Beckham scored a great penalty in the first half and the result was a stunning win that was one of the proudest in Sven's career. We were all hugging each other and there was a floating sense of disbelief, like walking on air. This was the first tournament win over Argentina since the almost mythical year of 1966. I think people forgot, after the dreadful disappointment of Germany 2006, that during Sven's first nine months of management, England had been transformed from nothing into one of the best teams in the world, securing two of the finest wins ever.

The next match, against Nigeria, was a non-event, but the draw we achieved was vital. The weather was amazingly warm and humid and the match took place at 2 p.m., the height of the day. For Nigeria it might have felt like a home match, but even in the stands I was wilting badly in the 40-degree heat. Sven was content with his progress through the Group of Death – an achievement that many doubters had found hard to believe. Then against Denmark we had an unexpectedly easy victory at three–nil. The next big surprise was the defeat of Italy by South Korea. Sven and I could hardly believe it – the wily Italians going down to virtual novices. For Sven this opened the door to the World Cup dream. He knew if England could just beat Brazil – with Italy, France and Argentina out of the running – there would never be a better chance of winning the Cup. The Germans were still in, but England had already seen them off in Munich.

Many regarded the England versus Brazil match as the real World Cup final and believed that this game would be the match of the tournament. I asked Sven to obtain the match ball and ask players from both teams to sign their names on it as a Truce 'Peace Ball' to go round the world to help war-affected children. I know that this was a very uncomfortable effort for him to make, but none the less he did it, for me and for Truce. This was the ball that Secretary General Kofi Annan kicked off to mark the UN International Day of Peace in 2003.

The Shizuoka Stadium is a very impressive piece of modern architecture set in the most beautiful forest country-side. At this stage of the tournament, the FA had flown out the team's wives and families to be present for the big day. I met up with Sven's daughter, Lina, who had just flown in from the American School in Florence, and she and Johan and I all went to the game together. The weather was fantastic and we had a full house from England. There was a healthy respect between the two sides, who knew each other well. As usual, Sven was evaluating the strengths and weaknesses of the injured players. In spite of a Michael Owen goal in the first half, Brazil scored two of their own. The relentless passage of time showed no mercy and England just faded away and out of the World Cup.

Deep within, Sven was absolutely inconsolable, although he would never show it. Johan, Lina and I looked at each other in disbelief. They had only just arrived and now it would be time to go back. When I was introduced to Prince Andrew after the match he said that he hadn't even unpacked his bags yet. Sadly, he wouldn't have to. I looked around at all the wives and families. They were all over the place – stunned – with nobody quite knowing where to go or what to do. There was never such a clearance of top teams as in this World Cup and never such a great chance for England to win. As I reflected on the passage of our year in England, I knew Sven would need time to get over his disappointment.

The collective deflation after losing in such a way was depressing. There was a sense of emptiness as the adrenalin of the last three weeks ebbed away. But if you are surrounded by other people you have to act as if you know what you are doing and where you are going. No one was prepared for departure because we were so full of hope that we would win the match; we were not at all prepared for the eventuality that we might lose. Consequently, everything was last minute and a rush. Those who had just arrived, having come halfway round the world, were about to go straight back. The frantic packing was a nightmare for us women in the group, since we had all been tempted by the requisite Far East shopping and had far more to take back than we had brought out. But our problems with packing were nothing compared with the looks on the players' faces. As we headed for the airport, it seemed that life was unfair. But, then, is it ever fair? I wished I could have made it better for them.

I wished I could have made it better for Sven as well. Going to face the media with Paul Newman, the FA Director of Communications, must have been so hard. The one thing about Sven is that he is a veteran of winning and losing. He knows you can't take it personally. Although football is a game of skill, it is also a game of chance. You can't have so much ego that you think you are always going to win. And you must be able to lose with dignity. Sven knew this very well and part of his coolness under fire is that he has seen it all. Although it may seem like life and death – especially if you invest all your hopes and dreams in it – it is, after all, only a game. In spite of getting further than expected, we both knew that England's being knocked out would renew the inevitable speculation over Sven's future. The football rumour machine would go into overdrive and our lives would be under the microscope again. There was always talk about Sven and club management, but he had not given up his ambitions for England yet.

THE NOT-SO-BEAUTIFUL GAME

●

*I have seen people behave badly with great morality and
I note every day that integrity has no need of rules.*

ALBERT CAMUS

XI OF COURSE NO ONE WAS HAPPY TO BE OUT OF THE World Cup. On the journey home nobody felt much like talking; we were all deep in thought about what might have been. It was over, but life had to go on. It was Tord Grip who broke the silence. He had brought his accordion with him and decided that what we needed was a good old sing-song. So there we all were, a band of not-so-happy travellers, sailing through the skies and singing at the top of our voices. It helped to dispel the gloom and certainly lifted our spirits. After that, a sense of calm and serenity descended upon me; in fact we all became philosophical, recognizing that there would be other opportunities.

When we arrived back in England, I reflected on the good aspects of a World Cup in a country where correct behaviour and politeness are sacred. There had not been the usual opportunities for fans to go on drinking sprees as they so often do in European cities, and there were not many bar stools or café chairs to hurl at one another. The Japanese police looked like Samurai warriors and were definitely not to be messed with. I was amazed at how the old-fashioned oriental hospitality dispelled aggression. This is the great lesson in manners. It is not about which end to crack open a boiled egg, but about knowing what to do and how to behave in different social circumstances. If there is a way of doing things, then conforming to it takes away the stress of not knowing what to do. Manners are like the rules of the game that stop a football match becoming a brawl. I began to see how the social cohesion of Japanese society had given us a very non-violent World Cup and felt there were lessons there to be incorporated in the Truce campaign. I was looking for a new code of chivalry, a *bushido* for the modern world.

I have to say that I was philosophical about the England defeat. There is no shame in losing to Brazil; given a different roll of the dice it might have been them heading home just like Argentina were. There was much analysis of the overall underperformance of so many of the A-list teams in this World Cup, with the general consensus allocating blame to playing too much football. In the heat, after a hard season and with all the nerves involved, the stress on players is immense. England's was the youngest World Cup squad and their loss to Brazil was their first competitive defeat of Sven's regime.

The English summer seemed to be an endless round of hand-wringing and picking over the fragments of the broken dream. In fact, in reaching the quarter-finals England had done much better than expected. The FA had had a five-year plan to win the World Cup in 2006. And, before Sven's appointment, England was doing so badly that they were not expected even to qualify for the 2002 Cup; this was reflected in his contract, which did not require qualification for Japan 2002. But Sven believed in his players and had been determined to succeed. I think people forget how rapid the turnaround had been from a side with little hope to one of the highest-rated teams in the tournament. I was beginning to find the pundits and the politics of football oppressive. This was not what summer was about for me. I felt it was all too much and, with a friendly against Portugal coming up in early September, I decided to steal away to soak up some Mediterranean sunshine. I would join Sven later for a spell in Sweden before going on to Greece for a week's cruise of the islands.

After the intensity of the World Cup it was great to be in Rome again. I went straight to our beach house at Fregene and was delighted to be able to sit out on the terrace and hear the sound of the sea. For me the sea is essential. I have an almost physical need to spend time there – it's both energizing and relaxing at the same time. There's something about the endless rise and fall of the waves that soothes my soul. As the sun went down I could see the fishing boats silhouetted against the skyline. I thought to myself that life is a little like the horizon: every time you think you're reaching the limit of your vision there is still more to see. Jerry had done a fabulous job with the finishing touches in the house and the rich combination of timbers and decorative woods gave it a warm, cosy feeling. Our master bedroom opens on to the upstairs terrace and we have a hot tub in the en-suite bathroom. On summer nights I can roll back the sliding doors and have the sea breeze and the stars for company either in bed or in the bath. At times like these I have to pinch myself and remember that there are others for whom life is not so blessed.

When we returned at the end of the summer I knew Sven's time would be wholly caught up with the tight schedule of back-to-back fixtures facing him in the challenge to qualify for Euro 2004. I had been a keen observer of his matches since we fell in love, and perhaps because it was all so new for me I had gone to most of his home games and important matches. This is not common amongst football wives and girlfriends, most of whom look after their families like anybody else. Now, the sheer scale of the English game, Sven's exhausting schedule of match attendance and his role as manager of the national team had made it more difficult for me to attend so many of his games. For the first time I decided to make a more conscious use of my time for pursuing my own dream of football as a force for peace. I had been thrust into the media spotlight by the high-profile nature of my relationship with the England manager, but I was also an independent woman in my own right. I have always believed that true partnership requires equal partners and Sven has always given me that respect. But that is not the way the media often portray things. I had no intention of being my partner's understudy, but I was happy to use my new media profile for a good cause.

In early October I had to endure further tabloid attention when Ulrika Jonsson's book was published. It seemed as though the Jonsson camp were looking to capitalize on their media property and the release of this sad confessional looked to me as though it was timed to piggyback on England's football mania of that summer. The whole sorry saga was fanned by the *Daily Mail* to promote its serialization of the book. Although Sven had reassured the FA that nothing of any significance would emerge, the whole of Soho Square had the jitters as the media hype mounted. In the end, the desperate project was overshadowed by events on the football field, with reports of 'monkey noises' being directed at England's black players by racist fans in Bratislava. I was very glad we won.

Also in October an invitation arrived for the World Cup squad and their partners to attend a reception at Number 10 Downing Street. I was hugely excited to be going. Of course, I had met the Prime Minister at the House of Commons earlier in the year and it would be great to have a further opportunity to talk to him, especially as he had been so positive about Truce. For the evening I chose to wear an outfit that became famous in its own right – my red catsuit by the lovely Kruszynska sisters.

Travel to the reception had been coordinated for me by the FA via Sven's driver at the time, Jonathan, who had been instructed to bring me to the front entrance of Downing Street whilst the squad bus arrived at the rear entrance. Going through the security checks, I enjoyed the cheerful banter with the staff. As I emerged into the half-light and began to walk towards the black front door of Number 10, I saw that the photographers and journalists stationed outside were stood down and relaxing. I was a solitary figure as I began to stroll forwards. Most of the press were round at the rear to meet the squad bus, so there was a buzz of anticipation from the small assembly at the front when they saw me walk towards them. At first they couldn't make out who I was, and then as they unslung cameras just in case, the cry went up. 'It's Nancy!' The pack of photographers surged towards me as close as they could get and I was caught in the flashlights until I knocked on the door to be ushered inside.

As I accustomed myself to my surroundings in the entrance hall, and was led in the direction of the reception, I glanced at my watch and noticed that I was slightly late. I picked up my pace and virtually collided with the tall figure of the Prime Minister. He recognized me immediately and, with a broad smile, and said, 'Hello, Nancy – how nice to see you again. Wow! You look wonderful tonight.'

With great charm he led me into the assembled reception and the first person we saw was Sven. I could see that quizzical look in Sven's eye as if to say, 'How does she do it?' I wondered if a blend of admiration and exasperation was going through his mind, as though I might deliberately have engineered the situation or even taken advantage of my position as his partner. This was all mixed up with his being genuinely pleased to see me; pride in my being his partner and looking so good; liking and yet resenting the appreciative glances of others. Heaven help women in the face of the insecurity of men!

Before he left us to circulate, the Prime Minister asked me about the Truce campaign and mentioned the possibility of hosting a reception at Downing Street. I was really pleased that he had brought up the subject of Truce of his own accord, as it showed that the idea must have struck a chord with him. After the surge of scandal, I felt empowered by all the kindness and support I was shown. This was a liberating evening for me and I loved the feeling that the genuine affection of your peers engenders. We were introduced to Cherie Blair, who invited me for tea, and to top the evening, the Prime Minister took Sven and me on an intimate tour of the private rooms of his office and residence. As I was leaving with Sven to join the rest of the team and their families for dinner, the Prime Minister said goodbye and asked me to keep him posted on developments with Truce. He understood the huge social power of football and wanted to be involved.

That season saw an escalating power struggle between the FA and the Premier League. Sven does not normally discuss all the intricacies of his working life with me; we spend as much time talking about poetry or ancient history as we do about football. We respect a professional distance between us that does not preclude a close support of each other in times of difficulty or crisis. The departure of Adam Crozier from his position as Chief Executive of the FA was one of these moments of crisis.

Adam was a casualty of the battle between the FA and the Premier League over matters of money. Throughout his career he had always stood up for the independence of the FA. His departure also had a direct bearing on me: I feared the Truce project was losing a friend who could see the 'big idea' and could have helped make it work. Having set up the cause-related marketing department at Saatchi's, Adam was one of the few people at the FA who could understand the benefits the national and international dimensions of our campaign could bring to English football. I had the impression that there were members of the football family who would not want to see us prosper and were envious of the popular appeal of Truce. I suspected we would now face an uphill battle to find a unified approach for a national charity project for football within the world of football itself. There was just too much vested interest and too many old enmities to be able to achieve what the entertainment industry had done with Comic Relief and Red Nose Day, or with Children In Need. Adam Crozier had understood the idea of a football-driven national television event to raise money for good causes. Others within the fraternity saw Truce as my vanity project, or as a competitor to their own pet charities. They couldn't seem to grasp that all their charities could benefit if there was an engine to raise a larger pot of money for general distribution. The idea discussed with the UN – of the UK being a pilot project for the world event – had stalled before it had begun.

I knew that, with his media background, David Davies – appointed joint Chief Executive after the resignation of Adam Crozier – would continue to give me what help he could. But without some higher authority than the FA my progress to mobilize national football in England would be blocked by those who walked the corridors of Soho Square in shadows. Sometimes I got a feeling there was a block of opinion that the partner of the England manager should butt out and do what women are expected to do.

I decided to talk to my friend Ann Taylor about enlisting the support of the government, combining this with a consultation with FIFA. The reasoning was that, by creating an international architecture around the idea of a football truce in support of the UN Day of Peace, we might be able to persuade the British government to facilitate a truce within the football fraternity.

The year was drawing to a close and the one thing that I noticed, as an Italian in England, was the dramatic changing of the seasons that, even in London, somehow seems more pronounced than in other parts of Europe. As the anniversary of the Christmas truce drew near, I wanted to mark it with an unusual example of football for peace. Our initial approach to the political parties had drawn a positive response, with letters of support from the Prime Minister and from Charles Kennedy and Iain Duncan Smith, leaders of the Liberal Democrat and Conservative parties at the time. I also remembered how Ann Taylor had introduced me to Parliament FC, the House of Commons football team. At the time I had been to a show game with ex-007 Roger Moore (I love James Bond) on behalf of UNICEF and we had watched the parliamentarians and the diplomats from the British Embassy slog it out. (I couldn't help feeling it was a bit of a grudge match. The drawback of being a parliamentary player is that nine times out of ten the opposition think you are fair game and in need of a good kicking!) The captain and officer in charge of the team is the Rt Hon. MP for Sheffield, Clive Betts. From the outset of the Truce campaign, MPs from all parties have given unfailing support and for that I will be forever grateful. On this occasion, Ann Taylor and Clive Betts came up with the wonderful idea of a fundraising dinner at the House of Commons in aid of Truce-nominated projects at home and abroad. We felt it right to strike a balance between charitable causes working domestically, such as the Variety Club, and those with an international remit. The MPs organized a fabulous dinner and raised £35,000 for good causes.

Sven and I spent Christmas in Sweden, as had become our habit – where better than the land of Santa Klaus? Of course, when your family ends up spread out in different places, where you spend the holidays is always a compromise. Sven is always keen to visit Sweden, particularly at Christmas, as his schedule allows him so little time there for the rest of the year. By now we were also very at home in England and our house at Regent's Park had become both a refuge and a centre of operations. With the Truce office at Chelsea Harbour and my corner table at Claridge's for conferences, I was ready to go to war for peace and wanted to hit the ground running in the New Year.

John Carmichael had known Dr Jane Goodall, famed for her work with primates and her campaign to save the rainforest, in her role as a UN Messenger of Peace and confidante of Secretary General Kofi Annan. Over the Millennium year he had worked with her international advisers, Mary Lewis and David Lorraine, and felt that the combination of Football for Peace and development could work well together. Sven and I had always admired Jane and wanted to meet her, so we decided together to invite her to his office at Soho Square for a meeting to explore ideas.

Jane arrived with her soft-toy mascot, Mr H, a gift from a blind conjuror. H travels with her everywhere, banana in hand. She is a very charismatic lady and had had the great idea of using football players of African descent to act as role models for her work in conservation. We may think of Sir Bob Geldof or Bono as well-known international media personalities, but in Africa they are virtual unknowns compared to most premiership players. Jane said if we wanted to influence Africa, we needed to have player-ambassadors to promote the campaign. She also spoke candidly about the frustration of the UN Messengers of Peace at the failure of member states to observe the UN International Day of Peace as a day of global ceasefire. Since its proposal in 2002, it had been passed by the General Assembly but then left to sit where all good UN resolutions get left – on the shelf.

For someone who is a confessed romantic, I can also be quite analytical. At the outset of a relationship people tend to be on their best behaviour, but as the romance turns to routine we start to take each other for granted. Power shifts in most relationships, unconsciously. Sometimes the pain of having to face the need to change is just too hard to negotiate. When you are the life partner of a powerful man, it is difficult not to be aware of his self-regard and his status in the world when making one's own decisions. There is a tendency to want to please him, to say 'yes' too quickly or to bite one's tongue rather than say what one really thinks. Since women are generally naturally more flexible and able to accommodate things, this can be taken too far. After the infidelity, I had became more assertive in expressing my needs and was more of my own woman. I had found a new well of emotional strength that came with having to confront the true meaning and depth of our relationship. After forgiveness and re-discovered closeness, problems can recur when external pressures mount and blocks appear in the once open channels. None the less it is important to trust, otherwise a relationship cannot mature into something of deep value.

There are different types of infidelity, just as there are

different psychological centres in each one of us. There is physical infidelity – the most obvious, because it is visible in action and behaviour. Then there is mental and emotional infidelity or, the greatest of all, infidelity of the soul. Even the best-intentioned of friends can drip poison into your ears – especially when parts of your life become public – but the only way to find the solution and avoid going crazy is to concentrate on the inside story that you know to be true. Moral virtue is not greatly valued in this modern world, but none the less virtue is a very important concept because it concerns the quality of your soul, the worth of your being and your value as an individual. The modern earthly paradise is driven by the consumer, who worships personality, image over actuality and style over substance. These things are not real, as we all find out when suffering knocks at our door, as it must do for all of us in the course of a lifetime.

Physical infidelity doesn't have to be the end of the world. It can be different for men and women. Women don't usually stray unless they are emotionally involved; men don't need an emotional attachment to have an affair. I do believe there needs to be fidelity in a relationship, but we can all be weak and make a mistake. It is the quality of your relationship and the depth of communication with each other that determines whether you can survive as a couple or not after an affair. Sometimes you grow up through the experience. Rousseau believed, idealistically, that human beings were naturally good. In his own life he was continually disappointed and could never find a true friend. I think we need to be realistic about human nature, in which there is both good and bad. No one is perfect and we all fall short of our own standards. This is why having the courage to forgive is so important. Only when you have hurt someone and found the need to be forgiven can you truly understand. Unfortunately, the modern mindset is so out of touch with the inner world of the heart, and the emotional blocks are so great, that as a generation we are in danger of losing our soul. The danger in becoming desensitized to one another is that cruelty has no consequence.

As 2003 unfolded Sven and I were both so busy that we had to be careful that we had enough quality time together. International football was again in conflict with the clubs, causing frustration for Sven, though he could see both sides of the argument. Although he says I'm absolutely crazy and that such a thing would never happen, I think Sven would be brilliant at high-level football administration. He loves the architecture of the game and the rules as well as being on the bench. As this is my book, I may be forgiven for stating that I believe that one day Sven-Goran Eriksson would make a wonderful President of FIFA.

The dissent in football was surpassed by dissent in the international political arena as the debate raged around the world on weapons of mass destruction and the role of Iraq in international terrorism. With the world about to go to war, Truce, with its idea of calling a halt to hostilities in order to consider differences peacefully, seemed more important than ever.

Inevitably, very few were really listening. 'What has football got to do with peace?' we would be asked, or we would receive wisecrack comments like, 'I thought football started wars.' Even the British government, which had proposed the motion for the International Day of Peace in the first place, had forgotten all about it. The build-up to war had become all-consuming. As fate would have it, the date set for John and I to go to Downing Street to meet with Cherie Blair to discuss the Truce project was the afternoon of the day before the invasion of Iraq in March 2003.

We arrived at the rear entrance to Downing Street to be met by Fiona Miller, Alastair Campbell's partner, who was then acting as Cherie's liaison officer. When you enter Downing Street it is a little like going inside Dr Who's Tardis: there is an awful lot more on the inside than you would imagine from the exterior. As we were led through the labyrinthine corridors we did not suspect that the War Cabinet was in session in the adjacent building.

We were met at the head of the stairs by Cherie, dressed in her tracksuit and looking very healthy from a work-out. 'Nancy,' she said, 'I hope you don't mind – I thought it would be nicer to make this casual. How about a cup of tea with Leo?'

The contrast between state rooms and the private apartment could not have been greater. We were met by a scattering of toys and all the signs of children at play. I love children (at least in small numbers) and Leo was a very charming distraction from the cares of the world that we all faced.

As we sat down to talk I could see that Cherie was distracted; underlying her hospitality, of course, was the tension of knowing what was going on in Downing Street on that particular day. Fiona began to take minutes of our meeting, but both John and I were aware that their minds were on other things and, as I tried to explain the Truce project, I felt that my words were being listened to politely but were not really hitting the mark. In the end Cherie asked what she could do to help, so I cut to the chase and reminded her of the Prime Minister's offer of a reception for Truce at Number 10. I think there was some relief that a practical agenda could be set. After that we could return to the more enjoyable matter of tea with Leo.

In football, too, the temperature was rising as the club versus country conflict continued. The fans were unhappy and the press was full of debate – some blaming the clubs and some the FA, even suggesting that the FA might withdraw the clubs' entries into European competitions if they did not cooperate with the national team on player availability. Sven is a very open-minded man and can see all sides of a problem – often to his own detriment. The conflict-driven politics of English football, however, were crippling the game and he was frequently very frustrated. He often bore the brunt of criticism for faults inherent in the English game and the way that it is managed. These issues remain today and, unless they can be resolved positively, England may never again reach the heights of 1966. Again, it is only my opinion, but the loss against Australia was a good example of the difference in approach to sport by both countries. The Australians have developed an integrated strategy to achieve sporting excellence and that is why they do so well internationally across the board. If the UK wants to achieve similar results, reclaim its heritage and maximize human potential, then the focus must be on the reform of the systems and governance of sport for London 2012.

On the Truce front, the time had come to brief FIFA President Sepp Blatter on progress and to offer the game's international governing body a football version of the Olympic Truce – the principle of working for peace through sport and the Olympic ideal – and the opportunity for a global fundraising project to help good causes. John and I arrived in Zurich on a crisp, sunny spring morning to be greeted warmly by President Blatter. Peace is such an abstract idea that it is hard to see how to make it happen. The core idea of the Football Truce was to stop the world for a day by playing football: the simple act of kicking a ball about for a day to honour the memory of football in the trenches of the First World War was enough to give teeth to UN Resolution 55/228 calling for a global day of ceasefire and non-violence.

President Blatter and his team at FIFA saw the very simplicity of the idea straightaway. In fact, when I explained that the event was called 'Kick a Ball for Peace' the President exclaimed, 'That's it! The essence of football is simply kicking a ball.' We all agreed that if there was any force powerful enough to make the world cooperate in a collective event, then it would have to be football.

At the time the International Olympic Committee was calling for a greater football component at the Olympics and we were also very excited about beefing up the Olympic Truce. One of the big disappointments for me in modern sport is that, despite the large budgets spent to empower the Olympic Truce and the lip service given by participating countries, the effect in terms of world peace has been negligible. With the FIFA Centennial coming up in June, we felt that 2003 would be a great year for the international launch of the Football Truce and that 'the beautiful game' might be able to achieve what the Olympics had not (or at least for a few thousand years) and put a stop to conflict worldwide for a day by the simple act of playing football for peace.

Finally, we discussed the focus for operations and, in line with our mandate from the UN to address the football development issues in Africa and the Middle East, we decided to partner on projects in Israel and the Occupied Territories. In particular, I wanted to look at the sites for FIFA's Goal project pitches in Ramallah and Gaza and to open a dialogue with the Peres Centre for Peace. We left Zurich feeling uplifted.

After my trip to Switzerland, I returned to Regent's Park to find the house empty and began to reflect on how little time

Sven and I had together these days. There was not much opportunity to ponder, however, as the time had arrived to take up the Prime Minister on his offer of a reception. Confusion surrounded this proposal from the outset. The Prime Minister had offered me a reception for Truce at Number 10 and I was under the impression that this would be hosted by both him and Cherie. Further to our meeting with Cherie, we were then told that receptions were only held at Downing Street on behalf of UK registered charities. Truce was not set up as a charity, so we therefore decided to nominate a worthy charity to be the beneficiary. I had heard the story of the tragic death of young Damilola Taylor and was impressed by the work his father, Richard Taylor, was doing with at-risk children in Peckham and the surrounding London Borough of Southwark, in particular the 'Mad About Football' project. Naturally, we were all hoping for a special fundraising opportunity with support from the Prime Minister as promised. Sven and I thought that by nominating the Damilola Taylor Trust as beneficiary of the reception we would also be helping to promote their work.

As things turned out, the event was a disaster for us and for the Damilola Trust. What none of us had known or expected was that Downing Street operates a system of tied caterers and charges for use of the facilities. To make matters worse, a complete press black-out was imposed, including a pictures ban. The reason given was security surrounding the Iraq invasion. I was extremely disappointed, as I'd thought that publicity for the Damilola Taylor Trust and Truce was the whole point. Surely a few publicity shots would not have endangered national security that much. The net result was to put a huge damper on proceedings, and although Cherie was a courteous hostess, the event was very subdued. Worse was to come, as the Damilola Taylor Trust found itself faced with a large bill to pay for the function. The fact that nobody knew about the event meant that both organizations failed to raise their profile and had to pay for the privilege into the bargain. I have little doubt that the donations made, which should have helped the work of Richard Taylor and the Damilola Taylor Trust, largely went to pay for the event. It was very disappointing for everyone involved.

Having hosted the delegation from the Afghan FA and the Afghan Olympic Committee at the Truce launch, we were very keen to support rehabilitation of the national stadium in Kabul. I had been very shocked by the sight of executions, including the killing of women, in a place that had been the sporting heart of the nation. The FA International Department was one of the key stakeholders in this project, backed by aid budgets from the UN and several donor countries, including the UK. Unfortunately, with the changes at the FA and the cutbacks in the International Department, there was a serious danger that the FA would not be able to meet their contribution to financing the management of the project's football development component. After discussion with Parliament FC, we decided to step into the breach and meet the shortfall with funds raised from the House of Commons dinner. I have to say that I would have preferred the money to go to a smaller charity than to shore up an organization as wealthy as the FA on what amounted to part of a UK government aid programme. However, we felt compelled to act as we did not want to let down the Afghan people over such a vital symbol of hope.

England's next qualifying match was against Turkey. I think there was a small minority in the country who took a perverse pleasure in hoping England would lose just to give a chance to be rid of the foreign manager; the Turkey game, which is always something of a grudge match, was one such opportunity. I was so delighted for Sven when his faith in his players proved justified. This win took England to the top of the group and they never looked back. But you can never have everything and, unfortunately, crowd trouble cast a dark shadow over the performance. The England supporters invaded the pitch and violence erupted after the match. This was the type of behaviour that Truce aimed to address through a new code of chivalry directed towards discipline on the terraces, with a martial-arts dimension inspiring young people to greater tolerance and self-respect.

Next, the team was due to go to South Africa for a friendly in Durban in May and I saw the opportunity for Sven, as a Truce patron, to deliver a Truce manifesto to Nelson Mandela. The evening after the team's departure I watched a report on their arrival on Sky News, which also carried a story on the players' meeting with the renowned African statesman. As I watched, I saw Sven standing with David Beckham at the head of the line to meet and greet the great man. In his hand was my monster Truce file for the Mandela Foundation. I stood rooted to the spot as I saw Sven, the first to be introduced, hand it over to Mr Mandela, who took it as if it was a loose leaf of paper and proceeded with the rest of the introductions clutching it to his breast. I had a warm burst of affection for Sven – only he would have such dedication. Some men would have given the package to an aide or been too embarrassed to carry it, let alone present it. That is Sven, and an example of why I love him.

The result of the South African friendly was a comfortable win for England, and then Sven and the players were due to fly direct to La Manga to join the rest of the squad for training in Spain. This was an important time for the players, wives and families to bond and Sven and I were delighted to spend a little time together again. I decided to host a barbecue at our villa; I enjoyed the chance to act as hostess and for us all to let our hair down together. When we returned to England there were just two more qualifiers to go before we could get away on vacation. I was looking forward to getting back to Rome and spending some time at our beach house. But first I had to rejoin the Truce team to prepare for a new initiative with MTV and Dame Jane Goodall as a precursor to the UN Day of Peace.

The success of entertainment-industry fundraising is self-evident. When the CEO of the newly launched MTV Europe

Foundation, Tom Ehr, set up a meeting to discuss a programme of music and football for youth, we were all very excited. Tom and Johnny had worked together before on UN-related projects and bringing together the 'Ball and the Beat' was an obvious next step. The result of the meeting was a plan to support the UN International Day of Peace on 21 September 2003 with a campaign of music- and football-driven activities focused on the star kick-off of the Truce 'Peace Ball' by Kofi Annan at UN Plaza in New York. The plan was for MTV to interview the England players as champions for peace and film the presentation in London of the 'Peace Ball' by Sven and me to Jane Goodall, in her capacity as UN Messenger of Peace, in front of Jane's 'Roots and Shoots' school groups, which help teach pupils about conservation and the environment. Jane would then carry the ball to the UN in New York in time for the Day of Peace. The project was called 'Play for Peace' and, as the lead time was very tight, we knew there was no room for delay. I was very happy to be fulfilling the promise made to the UN during our visit the year before.

Our June vacation was all too brief. For Sven and me this was just a little chance to recharge our batteries in Rome and take a brief spell on the boat in Greece. By now I had the bit between my teeth and, feeling a wave of support for the Truce campaign, I wanted to move forward to have something tangible to announce for 21 September. Gavin Dein, David's son, had introduced me to a rising Palestinian lady, Maya

Sanbar, who was the niece of Kofi Annan's recently retired Director of Communications. Maya was acting as the international representative for the Palestinian FA and offered to help Truce with the possibility of rehabilitating a football pitch in Jerusalem. At the same time Pini Zahevi, a football agent and an old friend of Sven's who lives in Israel, also offered to help with an introduction to Israel's Vice-President, Shimon Peres, and to arrange a visit to the Peres Centre for Peace just outside Tel Aviv. Obviously, Sven and I knew that Pini had been assisting Roman Abramovich with his acquisition of Chelsea and that Mr Abramovich was a keen supporter of Israel; it was natural for us to foster these links as part of our ongoing programme. At about this time Simon Astaire received a call from the BBC's Fiona Bruce asking to meet to discuss a *Real Story* documentary piece on Truce and my work in Israel and the Occupied Teritories. The upshot was that we agreed to take a documentary crew with us to Israel on our forthcoming trip to distribute kit and balls to Palestinian refugee children. We also planned to visit the FIFA Goal sites to see if we could add a football community development programme to help the local people take ownership of the pitch facilities. I was very excited to be realizing my dream. I felt as if destiny had led me through all my trials, from political defeat and a broken marriage, to discover my true self in a mission to help give back hope to war-traumatized children.

About this time the press erupted with the story of Sven

visiting the house of Mr Abramovich as though he had committed some crime against the nation. There were many reasons for Sven to visit – not least on my behalf as a patron of Truce. Of course there were tensions in his relationship with the FA and the change of management that had brought in Mark Palios to replace Adam Crozier. Anywhere else it would be perfectly natural to review life options at any time. We all do it. Sven had always said he could not understand why you had to be a saint in the England job. You shouldn't have a private life or earn money, and you absolutely must not look at other wonderful options in life. To him this was a matter of common sense and never once infringed on his loyalty to England or his dedication to his own punishing work schedule. I can say that no one worked harder for England than Sven, and no one approached their job more seriously or with more integrity. This was true throughout and until the end. As Sven said, 'Having a cup of tea with someone is not signing a contract.'

The MTV filming of the 'Peace Ball' presentation to Dame Jane took place at our house in Regent's Park. This was to be the first and only time that we would open up our home to cameras. We had invited along fifty children from Jane's 'Roots and Shoots' groups in London; she has a worldwide network of these children's groups and their participation was important for the world event to mark the UN Day of Peace. Sven's daughter, Lina, is a big fan of Jane's and was over on a visit from Florence. The day went very well and with the handover of the 'Peace Ball' came a promise from Mitre and the Pentland Group that they would back our 'Balls 2 War' programme to send footballs and football kit to children in refugee camps around the world.

As Sven and England progressed through the Euro 2004 qualifiers to top the group, I had little time to myself. Our visit to Israel was scheduled for November and I was thrilled by the support that was being expressed on all sides. With the ongoing work in Afghanistan, the prospect of a pitch in Jerusalem and the distribution of footballs around the world, I felt I had begun to make some small repayment for the wonderful gift of being alive.

The Truce 'Peace Ball' was kicked off by Kofi Annan and Dame Jane on 21 September as planned, in front of a large gathering of 'Roots and Shoots' groups at UN Plaza. The event was beamed out and synchronized with children's networks around the world. MTV aired the promo feature with the England players evangelizing the Truce mission and for the first time I felt that I had found my métier. I was fulfilled.

My next great adventure was to visit Israel and the Holy Land. This was a very important journey for me as a Jew, a Christian and with the blood of Saladin flowing in my veins. I longed for a way for the three great faiths to come together. In a way the violence at Sven's last match against Turkey was the decider. I had enormous admiration for the way in which this great Islamic nation has succeeded in modernizing and combining the sacred and the secular. Sven knew this game was vital – and he also knew that the atmosphere would be intense, as the relationship between England and Turkey had always been explosive. He did have a peacemaker on the pitch that day in the form of the world's best referee, Pierluigi Collina. I was glad to learn that the force had been with us and following their loss the Turks would face the play-off. My thoughts now turned to Israel.

Nick Mattingly, the BBC director of the *Real Story* series, had done a great job in setting up the background for the documentary covering my visit. The BBC crew were brilliant throughout, and in one or two tight spots when we clashed with Israeli checkpoints they remained cool as ever. A meeting with Vice-President Peres had been arranged and I was looking forward to seeing the work of his Peace Centre.

For me this was the trip of a lifetime. It was a true privilege to see so much as a guest of the UN, and the Palestinian Authority as well as the Israeli government gave me the opportunity of a unique overview. I was astonished to see the all-American Israeli boys managing the checkpoints, some filled with zeal, some reluctant, and others just plain embarrassed when we asked them what they were doing. In Ramallah I met a young Palestinan football player who had been shot in the leg; his whole career was in ruins.

Then there was the wall – this massive monument to division. I wondered how two such vibrant communities could stand the constant tension. As an outsider looking in, the wall seemed to divide a huge refugee camp from a huge military base. 'So this is what the Holy Land has become,' I thought and when I met with Shimon Peres I felt compelled to ask him, in front of Maya, 'How is it that Israeli Jews, with your history, can build such a wall?'

He turned and said to me, 'You know, my dear, this is what happens when two peoples are not prepared to pay the price of peace.'

I was touched by this wise reply – he was such an inspiring and charismatic figure. I was also touched later that afternoon when I visited the Peres Centre for Peace and saw Palestinian and Israeli children playing football together with their parents. I thought to myself that, if ordinary people can accept one another and let their children play together in peace, how is it that politicians cannot find a formula for peace in the world?

I know that Kick a Ball for Peace is not anything grand or complicated, nor do I think that by itself it can bring peace. But I do believe the example of the soldiers in the trenches shows us our common humanity and demonstrates how familiar things can bridge hostilities. If playing the beautiful game together around the world can bring about a day of global ceasefire, I will be content. The journey to Israel was an inspiration for me and for all of us who shared the experience. I would renew my acquaintance with Shimon Peres when I returned to Israel in February 2006 when I went to visit the football pitches built by Truce – the first ones in Jersualem where Jewish and Arab children play together. This first visit to Israel was my highpoint of the year and I was also delighted that Sven qualified for Euro 2004 and gave hope back to England and the national team.

SUMMER OF BROKEN DREAMS

●

Great loves too must be endured

COCO CHANEL

XII THE SPRING OF 2004 WAS A SEASON OF GREAT hope and expectation. I had a wonderful support team and the prospects for Truce were bright. With the negative events of 2002 well behind us and England having qualified top of their group for Euro 2004, both Sven and I felt we could look forward to an amazing year. Despite the determination of the pundits in the press to rain on Sven's parade, the atmosphere on the streets throughout the UK was fantastic. Everywhere we went people greeted us with warmth and affection. There was a belief at all levels of society that England, Sven and the new generation of home-grown talent could raise the nation to its former glory and fulfill the dream of winning a major international tourna-ment again. There was a resurgence of patriotism in the knowledge that this England team was capable of bringing home the European trophy.

The partnership between Truce and the MTV foundation was now focusing on Africa with the 'Balls 2 War' campaign, sending ten thousand Mitre footballs, donated by Andy Rubin of the Pentland Group, to war-affected children in camps in the Western subregion. As my media commitments and charity work grew, I decided to take on a publicist, my friend Giulia Constantini, to work with Simon and Johnny.

The success of the MTV relationship led to Tom Ehr asking if I would like to do some TV work connected to Euro 2004. I didn't think this was really appropriate. This was Sven's moment, not mine, and he did not need the distraction, so I decided to decline. Instead, as a spoof project, we did a series of football 'cribs' on the houses of rich and famous soccer stars. This was my first real work in front of the camera – it was fun, but I realized how incredibly time-consuming television is and how working full time in TV must take over your life.

I was also scheduled to do a feature on Truce for *Hello!* magazine in May for publication in June. It was so much fun to be doing this now. I enjoyed it more than I ever could have done in my twenties. Now I had the confidence not only to appreciate the attention, but also to direct it for my own purposes. I knew John Swannell's pictures would be just fabulous, securing the maximum attention and revenue for Truce. The photoshoot, in Rome, showed the city through my eyes as I tried to explain how the ideas behind my new cause had become so important to me. I thought the result was fantastic, but the feature came out on the eve of the quarter-finals and I think Sven may have been a little unhappy with this timing.

With the business in the UK wrapped up, it was time to think of heading for Portugal to get settled in for the tournament. I decided to stay at our villa north of Cascais, an equal distance from the hotel in which the families of the players were staying and the team accommodation. I invited Giulia to stay with me for a few days as the social whirl of the tournament began. In many ways it was something of a holiday for me. Many friends dropped by for lunch or casual dinners and I spent time walking on the beach or playing sport with any particularly active visitors. We'd only just finished the refurbishment of the Portuguese villa, so I enjoyed being able to entertain guests there. Whenever I go to Portugal I find the people so generous and the atmosphere so friendly that I feel immediately at home. Perhaps that's also because there is a flavour to everything, even the food, that reminds me of Apulia.

The opening match was against France and initially England looked as though they would win. Then the old magic of Zinedine Zidane stole the game for France and I knew English morale would take a tumble. But they rallied to give two quality performances, defeating Switzerland and Croatia to qualify for the quarter-finals. Families – wives and girlfriends – at the hotel brought a little normality into the players' routine for a few hours after each match. So far Euro

2004 seemed to have been dominated by the unexpected. Italy were out and Germany had been beaten by the Czechs. The path to the top had been cleared and there was a real chance for England to go all the way. All that remained was to beat Portugal. The trophy might be ours.

Playing the host team you can normally expect a tough game, but England's army of fans swelled the stadium. In the end the match went to penalties and the rest is history. Following our defeat, the atmosphere at dinner that evening in the team's hotel was sombre – adrenalin was starting to give way to anger and disillusionment. We slept for just a couple of hours before the team had to leave. I could read the frustration in Sven's face – his powerlessness in the face of England's loss. There was nothing he could do to change it now. I had decided that it was important for me to return to London with Sven, even though I would fly back to Portugal again the following day. I wanted to be with my man and his players to show my solidarity in the face of their defeat. Sven was very down and seemed distracted. I put it down to his self-questioning. Despite our optimistic start to the year, our relationship had become a little strained with us both being so busy; but I had not given too much thought to the effect the pressure was having on us.

We both returned to our house in Portugal and stayed there together for a few days. I could see that Sven was restless and at times like these I knew he liked to go to ground in Sweden to work things through. After he left I decided I would stay on at the villa with friends. Barbara and David Dein stayed over and my friend from Israel, Ghila, came for a few days. Then I would go to Rome. Giulia was also with me in Portugal, so we planned my schedule and took a little time to talk over my new role as an Ambassador for the Red Cross. My first engagement would be to attend a dinner for sixty people with the Chairman of the Red Cross, Nicholas Young, to be hosted by Prince Charles at Highgrove in his role of patron. I was really looking forward to seeing the famous Highgrove garden. I also had a Sport Relief slot on the Jonathan Ross show to publicize the work of Truce.

It was mid-July and I'd just arrived in Rome when rumours began flying around once more about Sven and another woman. I was told by my PR team that an article had appeared in the *News of the World* about Sven's affair with a secretary at the FA. My first instinct was to think oh no, not again. The constant press intrusion into Sven's private life – into my private life – was wearing me down. After the earlier scandal and the press coverage involved, I couldn't believe Sven could have put himself in this position again. He knew how badly I had been hurt already. Having just shared the shame of the national team failing once again to win a major tournament, I thought the press might be out for some sort of revenge and were just baying for his blood. Sven, at first, neither admitted nor denied any sort of affair and I wanted to believe that the story could not be true. We decided we had to meet to talk and he asked me to come to London. A private plane was arranged and I left Rome with a heavy heart, not knowing what to think or what to believe.

Once again the frontage of our house was a camping ground for journalists and photographers. This was like a nightmare déjà vu and I had to hold my breath to contain my emotions. Sven looked white and drawn as he led me into the sitting room. I listened to him stumble over his words with guilt and embarrassment. I could hardly take in the words – it was like a replay of the time before. He said that this had been a moment of madness. It meant nothing. What can you say when you know you are guilty and your job is on the line? I knew he just wanted to get away. I was furious. I had forgiven him once, but now Sven's behaviour was making us both look ridiculous and making a mockery of our love. Why would any self-respecting, intelligent woman put up with this betrayal? I had conferred with Giulia and I knew the newspapers were beginning to ask this same question. One of the problems of 'celebrity' is having to live every aspect of your life under public scrutiny. I know that there are lots of perks and privileges extended to those in the public eye, but you also have to put up with the knocks and constant criticism when things go wrong. Other people – people who really know nothing about you – feel that they have a right to comment on your personal situation, no matter how intrusive that might be. Some in the media make assumptions based on just the scantiest bits of knowledge – often little more than gossip – and feel qualified to comment on your state of mind. In a relationship that is private and not subject to the inquisitive questioning of the press, you can take your time to work through your problems and to make up your own mind without third-party pressure. I was in a no-win situation. If I made no comment, which I felt would be the dignified thing to do, I would be criticized for behaving like a doormat – which I most certainly am not. Although I did not want to be rushed into anything by media pressure, for my own peace of mind I knew I had to do something.

I was disoriented and I decided that enough was enough: the only thing to do was to take some time apart. I had to tell Sven that I needed a break from him, from all the press speculation and from England. He begged me to reconsider and to come away with him, but I was immovable. He wanted me to be close to him; I just wanted to get away. In a strange way I felt that he was like a child who does something that he knows will make his mother angry just to get her attention. Even the anger and rejection are worth the pain for the making up when the incident is over. I could not help but notice the serial nature of his fall from grace whenever tension was building in his life. Sometimes it seems that Sven has an unconscious ability to self-destruct. But this was a form of self-hurting I did not wish to share. I know it was said that I throw plates about. It's true that I like to get everything out in the open, but that does not generally include the china. Sven, however, can't express himself so directly. When he is down or depressed he can hurt himself and those he loves. He has always had a sense of insecurity with me. Even though I had stood by him in the past, he still felt the need to test my boundaries. I do not give up those I love even in the utmost extremity, but I needed time and I could not be with him in this situation. His bag was already packed – just a little carry-all – and once he knew that I could not be moved he gathered himself to say goodbye. We were both in tears again and as he turned to leave there was that forlorn look as, with his shoulders drooping, he went outside to the waiting car.

I dried my eyes. No time to cry. I was not going to let this mess get in the way of my life. I needed the time to sort out where I was and where I was going emotionally.

The next evening was the Red Cross reception at Highgrove and I thought Giulia would make a fine replacement date for Sven. I was looking forward to the drive through the Cotswold countryside to Tetbury; it would give me chance to take stock. I had dressed in a beautiful long, green floaty dress, which I thought would be perfect for the summer evening and the black-tie dress code. I hadn't quite bargained on the full tour of the gardens and before we had finished my hem gave me the distinctive look of a gardener. Even the Prince remarked that he feared for my dress. From the moment I was introduced to him, I was intrigued by how charming and charismatic Prince Charles was. We chatted in the garden and he congratulated me on joining the family of the Red Cross, particularly, he said, since my life was not easy just then. Later Camilla joked that I was giving her and the

Prince a break from the attentions of the tabloids. She was so bright and engaging that I could certainly see the attraction she obviously held for many men. Before dinner Giulia managed to arrange for one of the housekeepers to scrub the hem of my dress clean in the Ladies. Everything about Highgrove was a fabulous experience and the dinner was superb. English people don't really appreciate how lucky they are to retain the Royal tradition that has been lost in so many European countries.

The next day, before I flew out of London en route for Italy, I took a briefing from my press team on the latest developments. The situation was going from bad to worse. Sven will never comment on his private life, but in his absence the FA – having initially denied the story – had put out the most ambiguous statements, which gave the press a field day. I was aware that more details of Sven's infidelity were appearing in the newspapers, and that it appeared to be turning into a full-blown scandal involving bribery, corruption and other senior staff at the FA. Once again, it seemed that the woman concerned had been after money for her story, and that Sven had been taken in. Of course, the press were trying to get hold of me, too, for my side of the story. I was just glad to be going away and intended to make the best of a few weeks in the sun. By going to Europe, I thought I would escape the pursuit. Little did I know the extent of the interest or to what lengths the press would go for the story.

To escape the paparazzi I had taken a private plane to

Apulia from Rome. I couldn't even stay with my parents with anonymity. My refuge was a beautiful place in the Valle d'Itria near Fasano belonging to Marisa, an old friend of mine from my campaign days with Forza Italia. I arrived secretly with my friend Patrizia and we were expecting Giulia to join us in due course. This was a girls' retreat. It was bliss to get away from prying eyes and the constant attention whenever I had stepped out of my house. I spent the first few days by the pool, reading and relaxing. But my secret was not secret for long. Marisa is used to celebrity clients and the need for privacy and protection, but she had never known the attention that she would now receive. She said that she almost had a breakdown as she came under siege from the paparazzi. She said, 'This could only happen with Nancy!'

One afternoon, as Patrizia and I were relaxing by the pool and sunbathing, I decided to take a little swim and cool off. Of course the pool was off limits and under strict hotel security. Suddenly, as I turned in the pool, a glint of reflected sunlight caught my eye. To my astonishment I saw that one of the men sunbathing had a towel over him and a camera concealed between his legs. I made a sign to Patrizia to call hotel security. Then I swam over to the fat man and said, 'Is that a camera between your legs . . . ?' You know the rest of the line. He was sweating profusely as security led him away, having already called the police. It transpired that two paparazzi posing as tourists had taken a hotel bedroom and set up to try to shoot us by the pool. By this time Giulia had arrived and was shocked by the state of semi-siege we were under.

On another day, by the pool again, a woman approached me out of the blue and asked if I could do an interview. Giulia had to jump out of the pool to intercept her. As it turned out, she was another reporter who posed as a guest, this time set an assignment by our old friends at the *Daily Mail*.

The most sinister turn of events came when Giulia and I were on our way to a secluded restaurant in a small Apulian town. Giulia's phone rang and a man, claiming to be a Scottish literary agent, said he had heard I was doing a book and wished to represent me. Giulia tried to explain that this was press speculation, that he was wide of the mark and there were no such plans. At this the man went crazy on the phone and uttered the chilling words, 'You do not want to die on holiday.' He told Giulia that he knew our whereabouts, that we were being followed and he would be watching us. We were both really scared by this and when we got to the restaurant I decided to call Sven to tell him the situation and his security people got in touch with Scotland Yard for us. As we were outside UK jurisdiction they could not protect us, but they did recommend an ex-SAS officer who ran a security company and I later contacted them to provide security on the next leg of our trip, to Greece. As we left the restaurant that day, Giulia and I were starting at shadows, seeing menacing figures in the darkness and imagining all kinds of threats to our safety.

The situation was so tense that we had a police escort to

take us from the hotel to the airport in Apulia to fly back to Rome. From Rome we hopped direct to Greece to pick up the boat for a few days' cruise. I know this may all seem like the high life, and in a way it is – but it also shows that there is always a price to pay in life, be you prince or pauper. I asked my captain, Vanghelis, to make for the Cyclades and to keep us on the move, hopping from island to island in a bid to keep ahead of the press. I needed to be away from the world to reconnect with myself, absorbing the energy of the sea. We spent our days taking long swims and sunbathing, just listening to the sound of the sea and soaking up the beauty of nights under the stars.

One day our search for peace was interrupted when we discovered that we had not managed to avoid the press entirely. Unknown to us, they had found our boat and we were immortalized in the English papers having a water fight whilst swimming, and doing yoga. After that our mobile phones went off relentlessly. One call I remember came on a line from London with the rather nervous voice of Mark Palios at the other end. He said, 'Nancy, I am just calling to apologize and to say that I never said the things that were reported in the press. It was all lies and we are all betrayed by the turn of events.' I listened and said thank you. Then, as he was making his farewell, he said, 'Please give my best to Sven and apologize.' This was a strange thing to say. I could only respond, 'Mark, I think you had better tell him yourself.' I was just amazed that the governing body of English football should be so brought to its knees over a sex scandal with a secretary.

After Greece, we headed for Sardinia to the beautiful Hotel Pitrizza at Porto Cervo, where I was determined to put on a brave face with my girlfriends and party all my cares away.

The one great event that lightened my life during that traumatic August was the birth of my niece, Ilena. I spent a few days with my father in Apulia while my mother went to England to be with Fiorella. I returned too in time for the birth. Ilena was born a Virgo, like me. This wonderful ray of sunshine made up for all the other things I had to endure.

By now I was all but done with my self-administered therapy and knew that my Truce duties were calling me back to England after the summer break. I had put the Sven issue to one side for long enough. Now it was time for us both to see what we could salvage from the summer of broken dreams.

Giulia suggested that I should mark my return to London with a party. As it had just been my birthday I felt it was an ideal occasion to symbolize a new start. My birthday party was held at Morton's on Berkeley Square. I had wanted an occasion to say thank you to my close circle of English friends and to introduce them to my European friends. Both Simon and Giulia set to work to make it fun. Kate Enters, who was working as an account manager at Protocol, was also on the team.

My birthday the year before had been on board the Royal

Barge and we had taken a cruise to Greenwich. That had been a much smaller gathering of the inner circle organized by Sven – the Deins, the Davieses, the Platts, Tord Grip, Kay, Johnny Carmichael and Athole Still. As we went further up the river, Tord produced his accordion and began to sing '*Amore*'. We all took up the singing, with Athole performing arias and Johnny singing rebel songs from the '45 Rebellion. We must have sounded like drunken sailors.

At Morton's we asked Alistair McGowan to be master of ceremonies as Sven and I loved his comic routines about us. We had a wonderful evening, dancing until dawn; that night there were more than nightingales singing in Berkeley Square. Sven had to be in Sweden at the time of the party as his father was ill. I received the news that he was not able to attend almost with relief. I wanted this to feel like an occasion of renewal and it was better to be facing it full on by myself.

I had met with Sven on my return from my summer exile and he had asked me to review my position. We were living in the same house but hardly saw one another. I think he was worn down by his father's illness and when he asked me if I would give him another chance I felt my heart melt. The truth is that relationships are about what is between two people. What do they share and how do they communicate? Strangely for two people who have had so many mishaps, we really know each other very well. At least we both know we can live together and even though we are very different we miss the habit of each other when we are apart. We both knew we would have to take things gently and test just being together day by day. I think we were both content to let things be.

The UN International Day of Peace had come round again and this year the momentum was maintained with another event in UN Plaza and with the 'Roots and Shoots' groups around the world. Both the voluntary sector and the private sector did their bit to mark the day, but government support was markedly absent. The UN Messengers were concerned that the Day of Peace had become no more than a token themed day and believed that something must be done to remind the UN member states who had passed UN Resolution 55/228 at General Assembly to honour their commitments to observe a day of global ceasefire and non-violence. Perhaps the climate of the war in Iraq made this too hot an issue to handle, but in my book there was never a greater time for an international truce day. I knew the British government had proposed the motion for the annual observance in 2002 and had then done absolutely nothing about it once the ink was dry on the resolution. I determined to go right to the top and ask the Prime Minister about the forgotten Day of Peace and whether Britain might like to set an example to the rest of the world. I had been impressed by Kate Enters's work for Protocol and for my birthday party, so I asked her to become my PA. I was sure that her intelligence and energy would make her a great asset. Her first task was to set up a meeting for me with the Prime Minister.

Meanwhile, I had my first big Red Cross trip. Going to Kenya as an Ambassador for the Red Cross was the experience of a lifetime. I have always been an admirer of the values and principles of the Red Cross; I was also impressed to learn that 90 per cent of their staff are volunteers. My role was to endorse the preventative health education programme for HIV and Aids, and to visit some food and water distribution centres. During my visit I was able to fly up to see Lokichokio Hospital, the biggest field hospital on the Sudan border, which included many English doctors on its staff. I saw first hand the problems of refugees and the devastation that these wars bring. I spoke to many of the patients and was astounded that they felt so little bitterness at the hand life had dealt them – they were just grateful to be at such a good hospital. In spite of everything, they retained such positive hopes for the future and I appreciated yet again just how lucky I was and how important it was to continue my work. I know the trend is for poverty reduction, but somehow I think this is secondary to the problem of human security. Without human security there can be no real development. We are cynical about peace because we fail to address the causes of war.

When I returned a meeting had been set up with the Prime Minister to discuss Truce and the Football for Peace agenda. I took Johnny with me, as I knew he had been at Oxford at the same time as Tony Blair, although he didn't ever talk about it. When we arrived, Downing Street was very busy with a visiting delegation from Iran, and by coincidence the Burns

Report (on Post-Primary Education) was just about to be published. We were led through the maze of corridors and up flights of stairs until, after what seemed an eternity, we stood outside the door to the Prime Minister's private office.

When we entered, the Prime Minister stood up to greet me. 'Hello Nancy,' he said, then he looked over my shoulder and did a double-take. 'Johnny, what are you doing here?' he exclaimed. Then he turned back to me: 'Nancy, what are you doing with this reprobate? Do you know he had a terrible reputation at Oxford? Platform boots and white satin suits, as I recall.' Well, the ice was well and truly broken, and then he turned to introduce his private secretary, saying, 'And this is Phil Collins – not the rock star!' We all laughed and then got down to business.

I was looking for a way to persuade the British government to return to the charge on the UN International Day of Peace during the very important year of 2005 – when the Millennium Development Goals report was being issued. The UK would also hold the presidency of the European Union and later in the year would chair the UN Security Council. This was an ideal time for Britain to persuade other member states to fulfill their obligations towards a day of global cease-fire and non-violence. I suggested the UK establish a national day of Football for Peace in remembrance of the Christmas truce – a national football day when the whole nation 'kicks about' to mark the UN Day. The Prime Minister understood the idea immediately and said he would talk to ministers and see how they could help. He asked John to liaise with Phil and first stop should be to meet with Tessa Jowell and Richard Caborn.

Although our meeting was informal and relaxed, Mr Blair was very focused on the issues we needed to discuss. Once again I felt the force of his personal charm. I know that he has had a difficult time in terms of public opinion over the last few years, but I for one will miss him when he is gone. He has truly changed the face of British politics. I have had to admire how he has so comprehensively expanded the political spectrum of the Labour Party, driving other parties to the fringes.

The Prime Minister was true to his word and meetings were set up with Tessa Jowell to discuss the way forward for a national day of Football for Peace. We had met Richard Caborn the year before when John and I were introduced to a young Iraqi exile, Yamam Nabeel, whose talented father, Nabeel Yasin, is one of Iraq's foremost poets. Yamam was organizing a tour of the Iraq national football team and we were asked if we could help. So began a long period of cooperation that has lasted to this day. The Iraqi national team came to England for a series of friendly matches. They took on Parliament FC and an England XI for a series of matches and tournaments as ambassadors for Football for Peace. This project was undertaken jointly with the FA and our one sadness was that the match against the England XI was not shown on Iraqi television. The team was made up of players from Basra, from the Sunni triangle, from Kurdish Iraq and all over. If ever there was a focus for national unity it was that football team.

The result of our meeting with the Department for Culture, Media and Sport was to set up a Football for Unity project with Yamam to bridge the ethnic divide in inner cities. Given the problems that, in 2005, culminated in the London bombings, we consider we were well ahead of our time. Unfortunately, we could not persuade the government to develop an integrated approach to these issues within the time frame, and the opportunities afforded by a national day of peace to mark the international UN Day seem to have been missed. The campaign goes on none the less, and we hope that the British government and all UN member states will one day wake up to their obligations. There is a certain irony in a situation when governments profess to want peace then establish a mechanism for achieving one day of global truce, agree unanimously to observe it, then do precisely nothing about it.

One of the good things about being a celebrity is that you can use that fame to draw attention to good causes or people in need. Of course, there is always an element of self-promotion inherent in the reciprocal relationship between celebrity and media. But that aside, I am sometimes saddened when the gossip stories make the headlines but the really important things seem to get forgotten. I understand the need to axe a story without a good enough angle. However, if a story that draws attention to the plight of suffering people or highlights someone doing their best to make a difference gets passed up for a piece of puff, then it can rankle. I have two examples I would like to share from my experience with Truce. They occurred with two national newspapers over the 'Balls 2 War' campaign. This is not a snipe at either paper, but a genuine sadness at a failure to do the right thing by mixing agendas for the sake of a story. The first happened when the *Sun* ran their campaign for the children of Beslan and Truce responded with an offer to give a thousand footballs. There was a rush for the photo opportunity of me with the balls at Chelsea when the news was hot. However, within days the paper had moved on to other stories and never collected the balls. The children of Beslan had been forgotten. We all know the game, but this is not fair play. The *Sun* was not alone. The *Daily Mirror* was also keen to cover an exclusive story of three thousand balls going down to Afghanistan with 3 Para Regiment as part of their battle for hearts and minds. I made it clear that the article was not to be about Sven or me, but about the work of Truce. They came to take the pictures but never ran the story. Sadly, there were lots of disappointed Paras about to go to the front line who got the impression that the press had no interest in them. I realize that newspapers have to get the best stories of the day and I realize there are world events more important than me. But, for the men of 3 Para, who were risking their lives for their country, was it too much to ask of the 'People's Paper' to feature the brave soldiers in a good news story to boost morale?

Not for my part but for theirs, I can say this was badly done.

As I fast-forward the events of my life in England I am aware of how much this country has given me and how much I have learned from being here as an honorary English Italian. You never know a country until you live it from the inside, and I can truly say that I feel quite at home here. I have found the voluntary sector in England has taken over from the Church in terms of philanthropy and the British people are some of the most generous in the world. I think the woman who lost faith in her mission through being disillusioned by the intrigue of Italian politics has rediscovered it again via a football story from the First World War.

Sven and I were so delighted when, in December 2005, Sony Pictures, having learned about the Truce project, offered us a charity premier of the movie *Merry Christmas*, starring Diane Kruger and our own Danny Boon, which recounts the story of the famous ceasefire of 1914. I would recommend it to anyone to learn by the example of those unsung heroes and the power of a simple thing – like a game of football – to change the world.

Sven and I were proud to announce at the press conference for the premier our contribution to the building of a peace pitch in Jerusalem and the sponsorship of twinned Israeli and Palestinian children's soccer teams to be managed by the Peres Centre for Peace. The event was attended by representatives from the Peres Centre and from Team Iraq. I think this was the highpoint of the first part of my journey for Truce.

The words of soldiers from the First World War trenches show what a simple game of football can achieve and that enemies can become friends over sharing familiar things:

Since we hang out with the Germans quite a bit, they send us newspapers, cigarettes, and we do the same. Not a single grenade has been thrown or gun shot because if one side starts, the other will follow and we're so near to each other that we would massacre ourselves.

At the end of December 2005 we took a New Year holiday to take stock of everything and consider the year ahead. We chose Mozambique – a hotel in the middle of nowhere in a place that was wild and (whatever our mood) romantic. Coincidentally, Nelson Mandela was staying at the same hotel and as Sven had already met him before, he introduced me to Mr Mandela and his wife, and the four of us had tea together. The most memorable part of this was Mr Mandela's luminous personality – he radiated such presence and inspirational spirituality.

On our return from Mozambique, Sven was due to attend an appointment in Dubai. As it was such a quick turnaround from our holiday, I asked him not to go if he could avoid it. He did go, and of course it turned out badly, as instead of a legitimate business appointment the meeting was a sting set up by the *News of the World*. Sven's comments at that meeting were subsequently published by the paper and there was uproar throughout the press. The FA were furious. They jumped on what Sven had said and used it to force him to leave his position. This was an incredibly stressful time, both for Sven and me, as the storm raged around us. I couldn't believe the press campaign against him. Surely the papers would want to encourage him and his players to work together towards success at the World Cup, not drive a wedge between them?

At the end of June 2006 we approached the World Cup. This time there was a sense of heightened emotion about the whole competition, as Steve McClaren was waiting in the wings to take over from Sven no matter what the outcome. The English Lions began their World Cup campaign with a respectable win over Paraguay. Brave Trinidad and Tobago fought hard but were also overwhelmed. We then drew with Sweden in a tough game that saw England in the lead twice. Top place in the group and a place in the quarter-finals were secured by another stunning free kick from the captain, David Beckham, as England beat Ecuador. I knew Sven would view losing to Portugal in the quarter-finals on the dreaded spot-kicks as the greatest defeat of his career. It had all started so well. After being narrowly defeated by Brazil at Japan 2002, and then by Portugal at Euro 2004, this third defeat – and on penalties – was the unkindest cut of all.

When Johan, Lina and I arrived back at the Brenners Park Hotel in Baden-Baden we were all exhausted – emotionally drained by the tension of the day. The wives, girlfriends and family members were all gathered in the private lounge and bar consoling one another. There was still that indomitable English spirit, which says you never give up and you can always fight again. But there were few words as emotional exhaustion took over.

The first person I saw was David Beckham's mother, Sandra. We walked towards each other with tears in our eyes and as we embraced she told me that when they were coming back on the bus they had been held up by a terrible accident in which three people had lost their lives. 'That puts it all into perspective – it's only a game,' she said.

As I looked round the opulent period reception room, I could see the family groups – the so-called WAGS – sitting together talking and giving comfort to each other. These women and girls, their accents representative of towns and cities all over England, were a fine example of their country. There was no hysteria or tantrums, nor any of the loss of dignity that is so often reported. I think it would be very backwards to deny English footballers the solace and comfort of their families at a major tournament when this is common practice everywhere else in the world. My friends in Italy couldn't believe the ridiculous levels of attention we were receiving. The WAG phenomenon was purely a media creation. There was a group of young women spending a few weeks together in a hotel – of course they found ways to amuse themselves when they had no other responsibilities.

But they are very young and their lives are as full of compromises as anyone else's.

After a big match it is always hard to sleep. I wanted to be alone – so I said my good nights and retired to my room. The phone went and it was Sven asking how I was. After a very brief conversation we agreed to talk in the morning. I knew he would get precious little sleep. As I lay back on the bed I began to wonder about us. There was a distance between us, as if we were each in a different emotional world but somehow still joined at the hip. Now that we were out of the World Cup, our personal situation would need to be resolved.

The next morning I took breakfast in my room – tea and fruit as usual. The hotel staff were great. They had all assembled to see us off. We had bonded over the period and they had all been hoping for an England versus Germany final.

It was a beautiful day as I set off in the car to the team hotel on top of the hill to join Sven as arranged. Hard to believe that yesterday we had everything to play for and now – just a day later – the future looked uncertain. I felt that Sven was going into his shell and the coming months would not be easy for us. At times like this he tends to retreat within himself and breaking through is hard. Even harder as so much remained unresolved and unspoken between us.

Walking through the doors of the team hotel I almost collided with David Beckham. We looked at each other, unable to speak. What was there to say? We embraced with tears in our eyes. He said he was going to a press conference. When I saw Sven later he told me that David had been on his way to announce his resignation. I have to say that David was a fantastic captain and is a great Englishman. He does amazing work for charity and is someone the nation should be very proud of. I will never understand the way he was treated by the English football family after the World Cup. This is a man who has served his country gallantly over many tournaments; a new generation has grown up admiring him. He is an inspiration to young people everywhere around the world, yet in his own country he has not received the honour he deserves.

I went out on to the terrace to be greeted by all Sven's staff and the FA directors. I had expected Sven to join us, but he called to say he would like the two of us to have a quiet lunch together in his rooms. He would be seeing everyone else afterwards at the team meeting before the departure. When you love someone and know them well you don't need to talk. We shared the mood of quiet resignation and surrendered to the flow of time. We didn't speak of the future or of England's defeat, but just sat together.

At the team meeting the mood was good tempered. This was a room of experienced winners and losers. Steve McClaren made the address, then Sven replied and said his farewell thank you to the team. Then there was a wonderful presentation of a scrapbook recording all Sven's time in England. It had been put together by Tanya, his PA, and the rest of the staff and is a brilliant piece of memorabilia that he still treasures today. It was a hugely emotional moment and I couldn't restrain my tears. There was a general embrace between us all, then we left to get ourselves ready to join the bus. That journey back to England was but one in the journey of my life.

EPILOGUE

•

WHEN I LOOK BACK AT THE TIMELINE OF MY LIFE, IT IS AS IF I have lived many different lives. There is the infant Nancy, born in New York, wide-eyed and eager to explore the world; then there is the child, growing up in a big Italian family under the Italian sun, finding her way in the world and having fun; later there is the rebellious teenager, reluctant to conform and learning from her mistakes. All of these early aspects of my personality helped shape the woman I was to become: first the university student, learning about love and life in the adult world; the city lawyer and fledgling politician, busy making her mark and pursuing her ideals; then the wealthy lawyer's wife at the centre of Roman high society. Latterly, I fell in love with one of the world's greatest football managers, and love changed my life again. Each and every one of these earlier selves has had her day, then taken a back seat to allow an emergent new self to take her place.

The essence of each is still there, buried deep within.

The Nancy I am today is older and wiser, but there remains a little bit of that child who needs to be loved, that ambition that spurred me on in my career, and the courage that got me through the traumas of life and death, love and divorce. It hasn't always been easy, but whose life is? Recently, when I have travelled to war-torn countries and witnessed at first hand real poverty and despair, I have to thank my lucky stars. I have been blessed. I have a wonderful family, and have known what it is like to truly love and be loved in return. My life has been filled with interesting people and many amazing experiences and opportunities. There have been sad times and bad times – but if I were to die tomorrow I could only say thank you and have no regrets.

After the 2006 World Cup, Sven and I decided to spend some time apart. I was in a deeply reflective state and Sven was in mourning. For him it was a time of personal crisis. He couldn't stop reliving the events in his head and he couldn't speak about them either. We had reached an impasse. I needed to review my life and we both needed more time to be alone. My charity work was ongoing and invitations were coming in for media work in Italy. The Italian media is always interested in Italians who attain international celebrity abroad. And, although I had not set out to make myself famous, my life in England had become a phenomenon across Europe and the world. I was still in search of myself and we both thought that we should give ourselves the space and time to choose what we really wanted.

Epilogue

We met for a week together in Portugal at the end of August 2006, but it raised more questions than it answered. But our split was not a separation. We still retained the same passionate intensity and the bond we had always had. We just couldn't express it. We found it hard to trust each other and hard to trust our inner selves. We could not walk this emotional maze together. I did not want to start the split but, once the split happened, I found a new inner strength. We had put our relationship on hold to learn to live again and find a new perspective. We had to find ourselves individually before we could find each other. At that point we were both lost. Of course there was risk, but this was a risk we had to take. We had not discounted the possibility that there might be others, but neither of us was seeking other company. I could see that Sven had not finished his own intensive self-examination and I was hungry for new experiences. At the end of that week we knew that we still loved each other but we also knew our self-healing had not begun. In order to grow, we remained apart for the time being.

In September, the season for those late-summer love affairs, I found my life reflecting my new priorities. As part of my interest in fashion I became involved with the designer Elizabeth Emmanuel and wore several of her fabulous outfits to different charity events. In addition to working hard for Truce, I was now travelling often between London and Rome, and appeared on several Italian talk shows. Among my new circle of friends in Italy was a kind and sensitive man who seemed to understand my emotional turmoil. He was very charming and helped me to centre myself, step back and understand that I was in a new phase of my life. I welcomed the chance to look back on what had happened from a different perspective. We hardly noticed as the friendship grew upon us and blossomed. We had let down our guard and, almost before our minds caught up with our emotions, we had the chance to become closer than friends.

Then it struck me that, for as long as I could remember, someone else had been my focus. For seventeen or eighteen years, I had always been in a relationship with a husband or a partner. Suddenly I was able to concentrate on myself and I found it a good place to be. I knew I would never walk in anyone's shadow. I was my own woman. There was a sense, just like the film title, of the incredible lightness of being. I had been looking for Nancy all along and now I had found her and made a new connection with myself. The only word I have to describe the feeling is the French word *ivresse* – its Italian counterpart is *ebbrezza*. There isn't a direct translation into English, although everyone knows the feeling of being 'high on life'. I had found a new *joie de vivre*, a walking in the air, that led me back to the light like my emergence from the coma; a clear light, like the one that shines from the eyes of truly great people, like the Pope or Nelson Mandela. Perhaps this was a moment of enlightenment, beatitude or nirvana. It was as though the pain and stress of the last few years were lifted in one moment of grace. Always forgiving others, I had not been able to find peace within myself. Ecstasy, rapture, bliss or heaven on earth; all fall short of this beautiful life emotion – *ivresse*!

My new friend was very giving and considerate. We had both been honest with each other and he knew I was already in a relationship. He made it very clear that he was looking for a serious commitment, but he knew my heart was not free. Then, just as I began to consider that this could be a possibility for me, I received a call from Sven. I think he sensed intuitively that we were about to lose each other, that I would be gone if he did not act to try to win me back. He said that he wanted to see me and asked if we could meet in London to talk. Although my new friend had always known I was not available, I think he was a little wounded to see me go. But I could not forsake the man I had experienced so much with. I had to give our love a chance.

When I returned to London, I had meetings to discuss the publication of my book and there was also a Red Cross function to attend. When I saw Sven things were strained and my heart seemed to be in two places. I could see he was still struggling with himself. He persuaded me that it was important for us to spend some time together and asked me to go to Sweden with him for a few days. I went, with some reservation, but the atmosphere was charged and Sven felt there was a change in me. You can't just wave a wand and make it all right when you have inner demons to deal with. I had just been back a few days and was settling into my routine between

London and Rome when he rang again and proposed that we should go somewhere right away from it all. I was full of doubts, but something made me agree. I decided on Australia – a place I had never been before. I love plane journeys and a long-haul flight is the perfect place to talk. We were fine on board, but when we arrived many tensions surfaced and I worried that this trip had been a mistake. I just wanted to get out of there. My heart, my mind and my stomach were all in different places, I was in such confusion. Part of me was sad for Sven, as I could see how confused and deflated he was by my obvious internal struggles. My emotions were tangled and I had to ask Sven to give me time, although I think I knew in my heart that I would return to him. I could not just give up on us when we were both wounded and confused.

The process of writing this book has been therapeutic. It's impossible to squeeze the many dimensions of life on to a flat page, but reliving my past was like a repeated reincarnation. It is strange to see your life laid down in print, enfolded in the written word. Sven and I began to pick up the threads of our lives, but were in no hurry. I had my Truce commitments to attend to, with the focus on Africa over the next few years. Ghana will host the Africa Cup of Nations in 2008 and South Africa will stage the 2010 World Cup. Truce will be working with FIFPRO, the international football players' union, to Kick a Ball for Peace, which will include Africa and the Middle East in a four-year programme. I have so many projects in progress – in television, design and with the Red

Cross. It feels as if a whole new phase of my life is beginning. I am still here and still living in London.

Once again I feel the call of destiny as I write from my study. I look out on a perfect spring day and can smell the pungent bouquet of the wisteria blowing in from the garden, as the tendrils twist around our balcony rail. The magnolia and camellia are over, but the garden is pregnant with summer and it is only just May. How very English, I think, as I pick up my cup of tea and muse upon my last words. I was thinking of some recipe for life, or a version of Nancy's rules for life. Perhaps the only rule is that there are no rules. If we want standards, we have to make them, and if we want the world to be a better place we need to bring about the change. I know that I believe in love and, if there is any force that can change the world, it is the power of love. And love springs up like living water from the emotional organ we call the heart. Again I felt that sweet contentment of being naturally high on life; this quality that sends shivers down my spine, the *ivresse* of inspiration.

And what of Sven and me? We are learning to love again. For us, love means having the courage to accept that we have different ways of expressing our emotions and coming to respect each other's way of loving, even in the knowledge that love can result in pain. I think our story is like a journey, or like a book, where every end is a new beginning. We both have new projects to uplift us but, most of all, we are continuing to discover each other. We have talked of marriage again, as we often have, but we are not in a rush. We have both been married before and have never felt we needed a formality to define our love. Almost ten years have slipped behind us, and I honestly don't know where they have gone. Lived with such intensity, they seemed like a lifetime as they passed, but – looking back – it feels as if it was all over in the twinkling of an eye. Births and deaths: the birth of my darling niece, Ilena, and the loss of my dear grandmother. But I wouldn't have missed a second of my journey, and if I had the time again – well, I would probably change a few things. But I would not resist my fate. Fate, or karma, is the happenstance of accident, our actions and their consequences, the laws of cause and effect that play out in our lives. I believe in destiny, but we can choose which path we will take through the power of conscious choice, by getting in touch with our inner being and the intuition of a higher love that can guide us to make the right choices. I know in my heart when I make the right choices by the sense of *ivresse* that is my litmus test for living.

So this is the story of my life to date. It is the story of my heart, which I have opened and shared with you. For me this end is my new beginning and the challenges go on: to bring about a day of global ceasefire through Truce; to find more media projects; and, in my relationship with Sven, to learn to love again. We have come a fair distance, but the road ahead is long, with many a winding turn on the never-ending journey of love. I believe the best is yet to come, in life and in love.

ACKNOWLEDGEMENTS

•

TO MY SPECIAL FRIEND, FELLOW TRAVELLER AND CO-FOUNDER of Truce, John Carmichael, thanks for supporting me throughout this literary journey. And to his wife Nicky for her care.

To Doug Young, my editor, for his unique sensibility, understanding and belief in my story. To Emma Musgrave, for her dedicated time to me and my story. To my irresistible literary agent Ali Gunn, who rescued me from the airport and who has been my agent ever since. To the lovely Kate Enters, without whose help, day by day, my life would be more chaotic than it is. To Alan Edwards who intuitively understood how I wanted to present myself, even before I had decided myself! And to Anna Gibson for her professionalism and kindness.

To Alison Barrow at Transworld PR for her tireless enthusiasm and dedication to promoting this book, and a big thank you to the Transworld selling force.

To John Swannell for the beautiful cover shots and for being a constant delight to work with.

To my father and mother, who gave me the gift of life, and above all for their unconditional love. To Jerry, my brother and first companion on the journey. To Fiorella and Bill, my family in England, and to Gianfranco, who is many seasons in one day.

To Giancarlo, my very special thank you.

To Lia for her spiritual inspiration as the guide on my journey; to Maddy, a special friend who helps me to understand myself; to my childhood friends Cinzia and Sylvia, with whom I shared the first tears of love; to Laura, and my lifelong friends Patrizia and Wanna, both very dear to me; to Ghila, Pino, Rita and Ninni, Federica and Enrico, and to Rosalba and Cesare, a special thank you to you all. For my professor, M. Lupoi, and also a special thank you to Maria Mamos and Marisa Melpignano. To Lucia, my nanny when I was a child, and to Mona, who looked after me so well during my years in Rome. And with sadness to my lost friend Silvia.

For Tord and Inga, and to the four who have become my second family in England: David and Barbara Dein and David and Susan Davies. To Ann Taylor, whose friendship has been invaluable and whose political example is inspirational. To Kay, one of my first real friends in England.

To Guilia Costantini, for sharing the good times and the bad. To Tanya Willington for all her help. Thank you also to Robin Morgan for being my friend and counsel. To Paul Newman for his friendship, as well as all he has done for me.

To Jane and Arturro for their personal service and great affection to Sven and me, and to Ali, their son, a very special person. To Terry, my driver, for his discretion and patience. To those who have looked after my appearance: Ahmed, Claudio and Sophy in London, and Rosanna and Paolo in Rome, thank you for looking after me and being rays of sunshine in my life. To Tani, my long-time companion on the journey.

For the Truce team: Maya Sanbar for her vision and passion in sharing my dream for peace through football, Simon Astaire for being there at the start, Nick Shipp, Steve Day, Colonel John Wilkes (rtd), Chris Wilkes for distributing the balls around the planet, Susie Smith wherever she may be; to Fernando and Deb for the development of Truce's identity and Yamam Nabeel for his constant determination to make a difference.

And finally, a special thanks to my treasured friend Fernado Ghia, who is no longer with us – a much missed confidant and advisor at different stages of my life.

PICTURE ACKNOWLEDGEMENTS

•

Page 1: © Eva Edsjö/Stella Pictures

Pages 2–8: all pictures courtesy Nancy Dell'Olio

Page 9: © Reuters/Kevin Coombs

Pages 10–11: all images courtesy Nancy Dell'Olio

Pages 12–13: author with Pope John Paul II, courtesy Nancy Dell'Olio; author with Tony Blair and Sven-Goran Eriksson © Simon Mooney at mooneyphoto; at National TV awards © Richard Young/Rex Features; author with Camilla Parker Bowles © Red Cross; author at Chamber of Commerce dinner © Richard Young/Rex Features; author with Jack Straw © Liverpool Culture Company

Pages 14–15: Balls 2 War launch photographs by Cpl Richard Cave © Ministry of Defence/Crown Copyright; Israel trip © Craig Hibbert

Page 16: courtesy Nancy Dell'Olio

Background images:

Pages 2–3: Statue of Liberty © Tebenkova Svetlana

Pages 4–5: view of Positano © Alfio Ferlito

Pages 6–7: *Nancy One*, courtesy Nancy Dell'Olio

Pages 10–11: sea view courtesy Nancy Dell'Olio

Pages 12–13: the Vatican © Massimo Merlini

Pages 14–15: Truce International, courtesy Nancy Dell'Olio